Crochet Collection
Wonderful Projects for the
Entire Family

Copyright 2016 by the publisher - All rights reserved.

This document is geared towards providing exact and reliable information in regards to the topic and issue covered. The publication is sold with the idea that the publisher is not required to render accounting, officially permitted, or otherwise, qualified services. If advice is necessary, legal or professional, a practiced individual in the profession should be ordered.

From a Declaration of Principles which was accepted and approved equally by a Committee of the American Bar Association and a Committee of Publishers and Associations.

In no way is it legal to reproduce, duplicate, or transmit any part of this document in either electronic means or in printed format. Recording of this publication is strictly prohibited and any storage of this document is not allowed unless with written permission from the publisher. All rights reserved.

The information provided herein is stated to be truthful and consistent, in that any liability, in terms of inattention or otherwise, by any usage or abuse of any policies, processes, or directions contained within is the solitary and utter responsibility of the recipient reader. Under no circumstances will any legal responsibility or blame be held against the publisher for any reparation, damages, or monetary loss due to the information herein, either directly or indirectly.

Respective authors own all copyrights not held by the publisher.

The information herein is offered for informational purposes solely, and is universal as so. The presentation of the information is without contract or any type of guarantee assurance.

The trademarks that are used are without any consent, and the publication of the trademark is without permission or backing by the trademark owner. All trademarks and brands within this book are for clarifying purposes only and are the owned by the owners themselves, not affiliated with this document.

All photos used in this book, including the cover photo were made available under a Attribution 2.0 Generic (CC BY 2.0) and sourced from Flickr.

Summer Tank Tops

Introduction

Crochet tank tops are the best summer time essential for a stylish, cool, and comfortable wardrobe. Why search through racks of clothes, or online stores for the perfect crochet tank top when you can make one yourself? It is cheaper than buying one and you can personalize it for a unique look.

Crochet is a popular fashion trend and these tank tops are will show off that summer tan. Each tank can be customized to fit most sizes with a few stitch changes. Now you can fill your closet with a rainbow of colorful crochet tanks for summer without breaking the bank.

If you are an avid crochet hooker you will have no problem finishing one or more of these tanks in one day. A few hours are all it takes to hook up one of these adorable tops. The patterns show step by step how each tank top is worked up. If you are experienced with crochet you can play with yarn weights and hook sizes to customize the look of each tank.

Crochet tank tops travel easy, they don't wrinkle and washing only makes them softer! They look great over a basic tank, or paired with your favorite bikini. They are so easy to customize with crochet accents you will never need to buy another crochet tank again!

Depending on your skill level, you can add shell stitches to add a bit of lacy flair, or a band of crochet ribbing and make the tank a crop top. A few crocheted flowers and maybe some crocheted tassels will add some boho style, or you can just loose a few rows of stitches at the bottom and add some fringe for a Woodstock revisited look everyone will love.

These summertime wardrobe wonders are perfect for throwing over a bathing suit when it's time to leave the beach for the board walk. You can make them in colors to match all the bottoms in your wardrobe and still have enough money left over for ice cream. They are great gifts too; everyone loves crochet tank tops because they look great without a lot of effort.

It is easy to change the tank top into a tank dress. Just repeat the last few rows of the tank top and increase a few times until it reaches the length you want. From here you can add patch pockets, crochet accents, or even some fringe and beads.

These patterns will keep you crocheting all summer long and keep your wardrobe looking fresh all season. Each tank is easy to do as long as you know the basic crochet stitches, that's it, no struggling with charts or long abbreviations. Now its time to get started and crochet some hot summer looks.

Chapter 1 – Guide for Crochet Terms and Hooks

Before you begin, look over this chapter to familiarize yourself with the abbreviations used in this book. The abbreviations are standard crochet terms, if you do not know the stitches covered in the abbreviations, it is easy to find an online tutorial for beginners.

If you are already familiar with the stitches listed in the abbreviation chart, you will have no problem crocheting the tank tops in this book. The patterns for each tank use these abbreviations and hook sizes. If you are unfamiliar with these abbreviations, there are many good crochet stitch tutorials online to help you.

Crochet Abbreviations

beg – Beginning	bg - Block
cc – Contrast Color	ch – chain
dc – Double Crochet	dec – Decrease
dtr – Double Treble Crochet	hdc – Half Double Crochet
htr – Half Treble Crochet	inc – Increase
rep – Repeat	rnd – Round

sc – Single Crochet	sl st – Slip Stitch
sp(s) – Space(s)	st(s) – Stitch(s)
tog – Together	tr – Treble Crochet
tr tr – Treble Treble Crochet	WS – Wrong Side
yo – Yarn Over	RS – Right Side
( ) – Work instructions within the parentheses as many times as directed	* - Repeat instructions following the single asterisk as directed
** - Repeat the instructions within the asterisk as many times as directed	[ ] – Work instructions within the brackets as many times as instructed

Crochet Hook Sizes

U.S.	English	Metric
14	6	0.60
12	5	0.75

10	4	1.00
-	3	1.25
6	2.5	1.50
4	2	1.75
B	14	2.00
C	12	2.50
D	11	3.00
E	9	3.50
F	8	4.00
G	7	4.50
H	6	5.00
I	5	5.50
J	4	6.00
K	2	7.00
-	1/0	8.00
-	2/0	9.00
P	3/0	10.00

Chapter 2 – Easy Breezy Summer Tank

This tank pattern is for beginners, it is easy to follow and the finished tank is adorable! The long flowing knit flatters all body types and the straps are wide enough to cover straps. This is the perfect tank pattern for anyone who is new to crochet; once you finish this top, you will want to start another one in a new color.

Skill Level: Easy

Materials: Sport weight yarn any color 5 balls or skeins. Hook U.S. size F and I. Yarn needle. Stitch markers.

Note on Sizes: This pattern makes sizes small, medium, large, 1x, and 2x. The pattern is for a size small, changes for larger sizes are in parentheses. Mark the changes for your size before beginning the pattern.

Size References: Bust Size: 32in. (36, 40, 44, 48) in. Length: 27 ½ in. (29, 30 ½, 32 ½, 34) in.

Pattern

Band: Using the I hook, ch 26 (28, 31, 33, 36)

Row 1: hdc in the 3rd ch from the hook and in every ch across. 24, (26, 29, 31, 34) hdc. ch 2 then turn the project.

Row 2: hdc in every stitch across. Now repeat the last row until it measures, 33 in., (37, 41, 45, 49) in. from the beginning. Tie off the end. Now overlap the ends of the band by 1 in. then pin it to make the center back. Sew one long edge of the overlapped band to secure both layers together. The overlapped section is the back center, and bodice stitches will be done around the joined edge.

Bodice: With the RS facing, using the I hook, join the yarn with a sl st at the center back.

Rnd 1: ch2, now hdc 122, (138, 154, 170, 186) around the bottom of the band then join with a sl st in the first hdc.

Rnds 2-4: ch 2, then hdc in every stitch around and join with a sl st in first hdc of the round. Now change to the F hook and repeat the last round until the circumference measures 13 in. (14, 15, 16, 17) in. then tie off.

Straps: Measure 6in, (6, 6 ½, 6 ½, 7) in. across the top of the front edge of the band and mark it as the center.

Right Strap: With the RS facing, use the I hook and with a sl st attach the yarn on the left side of the marked center.

Row 1: ch 2 and hdc 13, (15, 15, 18, 18) across 3 in. (3 ½, 3 ½, 4, 4) in. toward the edge of the band. Then ch 2 and turn.

Row 2: hdc in every stitch across. Now repeat the last row until the strap measures, 18 in, (18, 18, 19, 19) in. Then tie off.

Left Strap: With the RS facing, use the I hook and with a sl st attach yarn 3 in. (3 ½, 3 ½, 4, 4) in. to the right of the marked center.

Row 1: ch 2 and hdc 13, (15, 15, 18, 18,) across to the marked section. ch 2 and turn.

Row 2: hdc in every stitch across. Now repeat the last row until the strap measures, 18, (18, 18, 19, 19) in. Now tie off.

Finish off by sewing the straps to the back band 5 in. (5, 5 ½, 5 ½, 6) in. from the center.

Chapter 3 – Cool Mesh Tank

The openwork crochet on this awesome tank makes it perfect for layering. This one looks good as a cover up too, just add several rows to the last row until it is the length you want. The cool mesh tank top is great over a contrasting color tank and paired with any bottom you love. The easy netting matches any style and this one is easy to personalize too. Just add a few crochet embellishments and you have a one of a kind tank top that will keep your wardrobe fresh and fun.

Skill Level: Intermediate

Materials: Sport weight yarn 5 balls or skeins any color, hook size G

Note on Sizes: This pattern makes sizes small, medium, large, 1x, and 2x. The pattern is for a size small, changes for larger sizes are in parentheses. Mark the changes for your size before beginning the pattern.

Pattern:

Front: Ch 91 (103, 115, 127, 139)

Row 1: 1 sc in the 7th ch, * ch 5 then skip 5 st, sc 1 in the next ch (this is one loop) *, repeat from * - * there should be 15 (17-19-21-23) loops, turn the work.

Row 2: ch 6, sc 1 in the first loop, * ch 5, sc 1 in the next loop *, repeat from * - * across the entire row then turn the work. Repeat Row 2 until the piece measures 6 in. Then inc 1 loop at each side = 17 (19, 21, 23, 25) loops.

Armhole: When the piece measures 13 in. (14, 15, 16, 17) in. crochet a binding for your size:

Size Small and Medium: Crochet until the last loop then turn the work, sl st to the center of the 1st loop, continue with the loops and repeat the binding on the other side.

Size Large and 1x: Follow the binding for size small and medium 1 time then turn the piece and crochet back to the last loop, turn the work again and continue with the loops and repeat the binding on the other side

Size 2x: Follow binding for size small and medium 2 times

Now there is a binding of 2 (2, 3, 3, 4) loops at each side. 13 (15, 15, 17, 17) loops remain on row. Repeat Row 2 again until the piece measures 14 ½ in. (15 ½, 16, 17, 18) in.

Neck: Crochet a binding for the neck, crochet 4 loops then turn the work and sl st to the center of first loop. Continue with loops until there are 3 loops on the shoulder. Repeat Row 2 again until the piece measures 20 in. (20 ½, 21 ½, 22, 23) in. Repeat on the other side of the neck.

Back: Crochet the same as the front. Crochet binding for armholes as on front. When the piece measures 19 in. (20, 20 ½, 21 ½, 22) in. crochet a binding for the neck by crocheting 2 rows over 3 loops on each shoulder, do not crochet over the center loops. The piece now measures approx. 20 in. (20 ½, 21 ½, 22, 23) in. tie off and the cut yarn.

Assembly: Crochet the shoulders together: 1 sl st in the first loop on the back, ch 3, 1 sc in the first loop on the front, ch 3, 1 sc in the next ch-loop on back, continue until complete. Now crochet the sides together the same way.

Neckband and Armhole Assembly: Crochet 1 row of hdc around the neck and both armholes as follows: * 1 hdc in sc, 2 hdc in loop *, repeat from * - * and finish with 1 sl st in first hdc on the row.

Chapter 4 – Easy Tunic Tank

This flattering tank top is the perfect length and it works worn over a top with sleeves or alone. The empire bodice design is flattering on all figures. The empire bodice is worked with a different stitch, giving the finished piece a stylish look without adding embellishments. This tank can be worn alone or layered and it is a perfect look for maxi skirts.

Skill Level: Easy/Intermediate

Materials: Sport weight yarn 5 balls or skeins any color, stitch markers, and plastic or metal yarn needle.

Hooks: For Bodice- US 7 and US 5. For the skirting- US 8 and US 9.

Note on Sizes: This pattern makes sizes small, medium, large, 1x, 2x, and 3x. The pattern is for a size small, changes for larger sizes are in parentheses. Mark the changes for your size before beginning the pattern.

Size References: Finished size for bust is, 31½ in. (35½, 39½, 43½, 47½, 49½) in. Finished size for the length is, 23½ in. (24¾, 25, 25, 26, 26½) in.

Instructions for Special Stitch:

Front post double crochet- abbreviation- FPdc

Yo and insert the hook behind the appropriate "post", the post is the straight part of a sc, dc, or any other basic crochet stitch. Yo and draw yarn through, [yo, draw yarn through 2 loops on hook], 2 times. Now you will skip the stitch behind the FPdc you just made.

Front Post
Fpdc = Front post dc

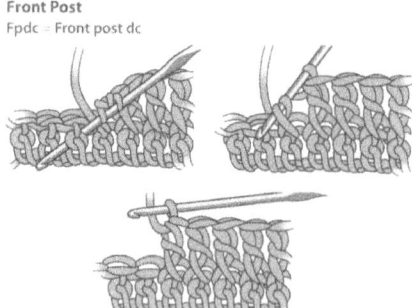

Notes: The bodice is worked from bottom to top in two separate pieces and attached with a seam. For the rest of the tank, stitches are picked up on the opposite side of the fabric and worked in the round from the waist to the hem.

Pattern:

Back of Bodice: Using crochet hook 5, ch 64 (72, 80, 88, 96, 108)

Row 1: sc in the second chain from the hook, and in every chain across. Turn, sc 63 (71, 79, 87, 95, 107).

Row 2: RS facing, ch1, now sc in every stitch across. Turn.

Row 3: Repeat row 2

Row 4: ch 1, sc in the first 3 sc. *FPdc in next sc 2 rows below, sc in the next 3 stitches, repeat from * across then turn.

Row 5: Repeat row 2

Row 6: ch 1 then sc in the first 3 stitches. Now *FPdc in the next sc 2 rows below**. sc in the next 3 sc, repeat from * across and end the last repeat at **, sc in the last sc then turn.

Now repeat rows 3-6 until you have 15 (15, 15, 15, 17, 17) rows are complete. Make adjustments if needed to keep the FPdc stitches in alingment with each other.

Arm Hole Right Side:

Row 1: sl st across 4 (5, 5, 6, 7, 8) sts, ch 1 then maintain the stitch pattern, continue until you reach the last 4 (5, 5, 6, 7, 8) sts. Turn, leave the remaining sts unworked—55 (61. 69. 75, 81, 91) sts.

Row 2: ch 1 and skip the first stitch, now continue across until you reach the last 2 sts. Sc in the last st then turn--53 (59, 67, 73, 79, 89) sts

Row 3: Repeat row 2, (5, 7, 9, 11,16) 5 times--43 (49, 53, 55, 57, 57) sts.

Work the estabished pattern until you have 32 (32, 34, 34, 34, 34) rows from the beginning of the armhole.

First Shoulder:

Row 1 (right side): ch 1 and work in the established pattern across 17 (19, 20, 20, 20, 20) sts, turn and leave the remaining sts unworked-- 17 (19, 20, 20, 20, 20)

Row 2: sl st across the first 5 sts, ch 1 then work in pattern across, then turn--12 (14, 15, 15, 15, 15) sts.

Row 3: ch 1 then work in pattern across to the last 2 sts, skip the next st and sc in the last st then turn—11 (13, 14, 14, 14, 14) sts.

Row 4: ch 1 then skip the next st, work in pattern across then turn-- 10 (12, 13, 13, 13, 13) sts.

Repeat rows 3 and 4 two more times-- 6 (8, 9, 9, 9, 9) sts.

Work the established pattern until you have completed 44 (46, 48, 50, 50, 52) rows from the beginning of the armhole then tie off.

Second Shoulder:

Row 1 (right side): with the right side facing, skip 9 (11, 13, 15, 17, 17) sts to the left of the last st in row 1 of the first shoulder. Now ch 1 and starting in the same st, work the pattern across then turn--17 (19, 20, 20, 20, 20) sts.

Row 2: ch 1 then work pattern across until the last 5 sts then turn and leave the remaining sts unworked-- 12 (14, 15, 15, 15, 15) sts.

Row 3: ch 1 then skip the first st, work the pattern across, turn-- 11 (13, 14, 14, 14, 14) sts.

Row 4: ch 1, now work pattern across until you reach the last 2 sts, skip the next st, sc in the last st then turn-- 10 (12, 13, 13, 13, 13) sts.

Repeat rows 3 and 4 two more times-- 6 (8, 9, 9, 9, 9) sts.

Work the established pattern until you have completed 44 (46, 48, 50, 50, 52) rows from the beginning of the armhole then tie off.

Bodice Front: Work the same as you did for the back of the bodice until you have 28 (28, 30, 30, 30, 30) rows completed from the beginning of the armhole.

Next Row (right side): ch 1 then work in pattern across the first 11 (13, 14, 14, 14, 14) sts, turn and leave the remaining sts unworked-- 11 (13, 14, 14, 14, 14) sts.

Next Row: ch 1 then skip the first st, work pattern across then turn-- 10 (12, 13, 13, 13, 13) sts

Nex Row: ch 1 then work pattern across until you reach the last 2 sts, skip the next st, sc in the last st, now turn-- 9 (11, 12, 12, 12, 12) sts.

Repeat the last 2 rows once-- 7 (9, 10, 10, 10, 10) sts.

Next Row: ch 1 then skip the next st, now work the pattern across then turn-- 6 (8, 9, 9, 9, 9) sts.

Work the pattern until you have completed 44 (46, 48, 50, 50, 52) rows from the beginning of the armhole then tie off.

Second Shoulder:

Row 1: With the right side facing, skip 21 (23, 25, 27, 29, 29) sts to the left of the last st made in row 1 of the first shoulder. Ch 1, starting in the same st, work the pattern across, turn-- 11 (13, 14, 14, 14, 14) sts.

Row 2: ch 1, work the pattern across until you reach the last 2 sts, skip the next st, sc ch in last st then turn-- 10 (12, 13, 13, 13, 13) sts.

Row 3: ch 1, skip the first st, work the pattern across then turn, 9 (11, 12, 12, 12, 12) sts.

Repeat rows 2 and 3 two times -- 7 (9, 10, 10, 10, 10) sts.

Repeat row 2 one time-- 6 (8, 9, 9, 9, 9) sts.

Work the pattern until you have completed 44 (46, 48, 50, 50, 52) rows from the beginning of the armhole, then tie off.

Assemble the Bodice: Using the yarn needle, whipstitch the side and shoulder seams.

Armhole Trim:

Round 1: Right side facing, use the 7 hook and start at the bottom of the armhole, ch 1, then sc around then sl st in the first ch to join.

Rounds 2, 3, and 4: ch 1 then sc in each sc around and join with a sl st in the first chain. Tie off after round 4.

Skirting (bottom of the tunic):

Round 1: Right side facing, using 9 hook, join with a sl st to the bottom back center of the bodice. Ch 1 and sc in every sc around then sl st in the first sc-- 126 (142, 158, 174, 190, 214) sts.

Round 2: ch 1 and sc in every sc around, work 14 (8, 6, 4, 4, 2) evenly spaced increases, then sl st in first sc to join-- 140 (150, 164, 178, 194, 216) sc.

Begin working in a spiral and sc without joining, continue until the skirt reaches 9 in. (10, 10, 10, 10, 10) in. from the begining of the skirt. Now end at the center back and sl st to join.

Next Round: Working with the 8 hook, ch 1 then sc in each sc around then sl st to join-- 140 (150, 164, 178, 196, 216) sc.

Repeat the last round until the skirt measures, 11½ in. (12½, 12½, 12½, 12½, 12½) in. from the beginning of the skirt. Now tie off and weave in the ends.

Chapter 5 – Sweet Shell Stitch Tank

Skill Level: Intermediate

Materials: Sport or worsted weight yarn 5 balls or skeins any color, hook size US G and a yarn needle.

Note on Sizes: This pattern makes sizes x-small, small, medium, large, x-large. The pattern is for a size x-small, changes for larger sizes are in parentheses. Mark the changes for your size before beginning the pattern.

Finished Sizes: Finished bust- 25 ½ in. (28, 30 ½, 32 ½, 35) in. Back length- 20 ½ in. (20 ½, 20 ½, 21 ¼, 21 ¼) in.

Note for Special Stitch: This tank top uses the shell stitch. The shell stitch is created by making 5 dc in on stitch.

Pattern:

Back of Tank: Ch 68 (74, 80, 86, 92)

Row 1 (right side): sc in the second ch from the hook, skip the next 2 chs, then shell in the next ch, skip the next 2 chs, sc in the next ch, repeat across 11 [12, 13, 14, 15] shells then turn.

Row 2 (wrong side): ch 3, 2 dc in the first sc, sc in center of the dc of the next shell, shell in the next sc, sc in the center dc of the next shell, continue across until you reach the last sc, now 3 dc in the last sc--10 (11, 12, 13, 14 shells and 2 half shells) now turn.

Row 3: ch 1 then sc in the first dc, skip the next 2 dc, shell in the next sc, sc in the center dc of the next shell, now repeat across until you reach the last sc, shell in the next sc, skip the next 2 dc, sc in the last dc--11 (12, 13, 14, 15) shells.

Repeat rows 2 and 3 until the piece measures 11 ½ in. and be sure to end with row 2.

Back Armholes: With right side facing, sl st to the center dc of the first (first, first, second, second) shell, ch 1, sc in dc, work the pattern across until you reach the last shell. Sc in the dc of shell 9 (10, 11, 10, 11), now turn and leave the remaining sts unworked.

Work in this established pattern for 13 (13, 13, 15, 15) rows.

Back Right Neck:

Row 1: With the right side facing, ch 1, sc in the first dc then shell stitch in the next sc. Sc in the center of the dc in the shell then complete 3 more shell stitches. Now turn the work and leave the remaining stitches unworked.

Row 2: sl st to the center of the dc in the first shell then ch 1 and sc in dc, now shell the next sc. Work this pattern across to the last sc, 3 dc in the last sc, (2 shell and a half shell), now turn.

Row 3: ch 1, sc in the first dc, now shell in the next sc, sc in the center of the next shell and repeat 1 time (2 shells) turn and leave the remaining stitches unworked.

Work this pattern for 4 rows then tie off.

Back Left Neck:

Row 1: With right side facing, skip center 2 (3, 4, 3, 4) shells then skip the next sc and join the yarn in the center dc of the next shell. Ch 1 then sc in dc, now work the pattern across (3 shells) now turn.

Row 2: ch 3 (first dc), now 2 dc in the first sc, work the pattern across to the last shell then sc in the center of the dc of the last shell (2 shells and half shell), leave the remaining stitches unworked and turn.

Row 3: sl st to the center dc of the first shell then ch1 and sc in dc. Work the pattern across (2 shells), now turn the work.

Front Piece:

Ch 68 (74, 80, 86, 92)

Row 1 (right side): sc in the second ch from the hook, skip the nex 2 chs then shell in the next 2 chs, sc in the next ch then repeat across (11 [12, 13, 14, 15] shells and 2 half shells) now turn.

Row 2 (wrong side): ch 3 (the first dc) now 2 dc in the first sc (half shell made), sc in the center dc of the next shell and shell in the next sc. Now sc in the center dc of the next shell and repeat across to the last sc, 3 dc in the last sc (10 [11, 12, 13, 14] shells and 2 half shells), now turn.

Row 3: ch 1 then sc in the first dc, now skip the next 2 dc, shell in the next sc, sc in the center dc of the next shell, now repeat across to the last sc, shell in the last sc then skip the next 2 dc and sc in the last dc (11 [12, 13, 14, 15] shells), now turn.

Repeat rows 2-3 until the front piece measures 11 ½ in. from the beginning. End with a Row 2.

Front Armholes

Row 1 (right side): sl st to the center dc of the 1st (1st, 1st, 2nd, 2nd) shell and ch 1, then sc in dc and work the pattern across to the last 1 (1, 1, 2, 2) shells. Now sc in the center dc of shell (9 [10, 11, 10, 11] shells), now turn and leave the remaining stitches unworked.

Work the pattern for 3 more rows.

Front Left Neck:

Row 1 (right side): ch 1 the sc in the first dc and shell in the next sc, sc in the center dc of the next shell, repeat 2 times (3 shells), turn and leave the remaining stitches unworked.

Row 2: sl st to the center of the dc of the first shell, now ch 1 and sc in dc, shell in the next sc and work the pattern across to the last sc, 3 dc in the last sc (2 shells and a half shell), turn the work.

Row 3: ch 1 and sc in the first dc, shell in the next sc and sc in the center dc of the next shell, repeat once (2 shells), now turn and leave the remaining stitches unworked.

Work the pattern for 14 (14, 14, 16, 16) more rows and then tie off.

Right Neck:

Row 1: with the right side facing, skip the center 2 (3, 4, 3, 4) shells then skip the next sc, now join the yarn in the center dc of the next shell, ch 1 and sc in dc, now work the pattern across (3 shells) and turn.

Row 2: ch 2 (first dc) and 2 dc in the first sc, now work the pattern across to the last shell, then sc in the center dc of the last shell (2 shells and a half shell), now turn and leave the remaining stitches unworked.

Row 3: sl st to the center dc of the first shell and ch 1, then sc in dc and work pattern across (2 shells), turn the work.

Work the established pattern for 14 (14, 14, 16, 16) more rows then tie off.

Assemble:

With the right sides facing, use the yarn needle and yarn to sew the front to the back across the shoulders with a whip stitch.

At the lower edge of each side, match stitches across the side edges and sew the side seams from the edge to the armholes.

With the right sides facing, join the yarn in the side seam at the lower edge of one armhole, ch1 the sc around the entire armhole then sl st in the first sc to join, now tie off.

Repeat the armhole edge around the other armhole.

Conclusion

Now you have a few editions for you summer wardrobe and these tanks go with everything. The skills you have picked up for creating these tank tops will take you into your next project and beyond! Each pattern is unique and you can dress them up or down, add extra rows at the bottom to create a tank dress or loose a few rows at the bottom for a crop tank.

The cleaning and care of your new garments depends on the yarn you choose. Always follow the manufacturer's instructions for washing, this is located on the wrap around the yarn. Some yarns like sport yarn are easy care, wools may need dry cleaning. Your new tank tops must be folded and stored, never hang them by the shoulders; the yarn makes the item a bit heavy and it will stretch out of shape.

Just think! Now you have the skills and the patterns to dress yourself and anyone else in style. It is time to learn a bit of embellishing skill so you can dress up those one of a kind tanks and make a fashion statement on the beach, boardwalk, or out on the town.

Crochet Mug Cozies

Chapter 1 – Crochet Basics

Crochet is fundamentally a technique that uses a specific tool called a crochet hook that turns yarn – or fibers – into a textured or patterned fabric. The possibilities with crochet are endless and there are patterns and eBooks covering a range of patterns including, crochet for your home, baby or pet toys, stuffed animals or clothing. Beginners should start with simpler projects that involve crocheting in a square or circle to get a feel of the stitches before starting more intricate patterns ass it can be very easy to get lost. You will find easy, medium and hard **patterns in chapters 2-8 to see you through each stage as you progress.**

Benefits of Crochet

Many people are not aware that crochet actually has numerous physical benefits on the health, mind and body and many of them are surprising. Some include:

- Reducing depression – Crochet can be a way to take a pause from day to day problems and focus on the task at hand which can stop those with depression from spiraling and give them a sense of purpose which is often lost with sufferers.

- Reducing anxiety – focusing on patterns helps to distract the mind from the anxieties that you may feel and helps to give proper thinking time to come to terms with situations or thoughts that cause the anxiety.

- Relaxation – continuing a pattern (particularly long ones) have a mantra type effect on the brain and can relax you into a semi-meditative state.

- Stress relief – For those who are often stressed, crochet is a way to relieve that by working your anger out on the yarn and creating something with the stress rather than letting it overpower you.

- Learning a new skill – This is an obvious

- benefit that can mean that in years to come you can use the skill to keep busy, adorn your home and even save money on clothes and jewellery.

- <u>Postponing age-related dementia</u> – In a similar way to puzzles, crochet keeps the mind active and helps to focus it to use it every day which is a key factor is stopping degeneration related to age.

- <u>Creating new and intriguing projects</u> – These can be anything from gifts for a baby, at Christmas or birthdays or even just adapting new patterns for the fun of it. Either way it keeps things interesting.

Crochet can also be used for encouraging shy children or those with low self-esteem to be able to believe in themselves, as well as learn a new skill that can help with other areas of their lives in the future. Crocheting helps to teach structure and can also help those with reading difficulties to help to concentrate and understand how to follow patterns and rules while creating something in the real world to liken it to which can help them to understand and visualize.

Before You Start

Here are some of the main points you need to bear in mind before you begin:

- Keep balls of yarn away from pets or animals to avoid them getting unwanted marks or pulling of the fiber which can damage the integrity of your project. Completed projects are less likely to fray, more durable and easier to wash so ensure that you protect your yarn or incomplete projects.

- Crochet hooks and needles should be kept away from children because they may seem blunt but can pose a health and safety risk.

- Keeping a clear workspace and an area to store your incomplete projects will not only protect them but will ensure that you don't slip or drop a stitch accidently or without realizing which could jeopardize your project.

It is also noteworthy to keep: scissors, a yarn needle and a stitch marker to hand, for your projects and these bare essentials will help you during your projects whether a pattern specifically calls for it or not.

If the yarn type is not indicated in the pattern then use Worsted Weight yarn as it is the most common, middle range fiber that is the preferred favourite for knitting and crochet projects.

Basic stitches & Terminology

Beginners should note that patterns can consist of written words or shorthand depending on the difficulty and each specific pattern. They are interchangeable and are written that way to make patterns easier to understand while ensuring they are not pages and pages long. You may find that some of the following patterns have a combination of both as it makes viewing the layout easier to follow over one or the other. This is something that as you progress, you will get used to and you may have already encountered this method before.

Shorthand:

Here are the most common shorthand for basic crochet patterns that you may encounter in the patterns in chapters 2-9:

- Single crochet (sc) – the most basic stitch that you should use unless it states otherwise.
- Stitch/stitches (st/sts)
- Slip stitch (sl st)
- Chain Stitch (ch)
- Chain 3 space (ch-3 space) – Any number could be used here depending on the pattern, they are interchangeable.
- Treble crochet (tc)

- Half treble (htr)
- Triple treble (ttr)
- Double crochet (dc)
- Half Double (hdc)
- Decreases appear as (dec or tog) – note that decreases can also appear specifically to stitches, for example Sc2tog also specifies single crocheting two stitches together creating a decrease.
- Round (Rnd) – this could also appear as "Row (Rw)"
- Repeat from * to * - repeat instructions inside the asterisk
- Repeat from ** to **- repeat the instructions inside the asterisk.

Additionally, it is useful to know that within these projects a new line could be referred to as a new row or round depending on the context but both are used interchangeably from project to project.

To Make a Slip Knot:

Before you start your project the first step is to secure the yarn to your crochet hook. It is important to note that within patterns this does NOT count as your first stitch and the patterns are based on the first stitch afterwards (unless it expressly tells you otherwise.)

Starting by pulling a strand of yarn from the ball is called the tail and when gently dropped over itself, 5-6 inches from the end it will form a loose loop.

Place the crochet hook inside this loop and pull it back through the front end with the hook. By gently pulling the tail, the loop will tighten around the hook and you are ready to start.

To Join Yarn:

Some of the following patterns involve using several colours which requires using a technique to join the yarn together. In order to do this without dropping stitches or ruining your pattern is by joining the yarn at the end of the row if you are able.

You can also use this technique on larger projects that involve multiple balls of wall.

The easiest way to do this is by working your original colour until you are left with two loops left on your crochet hook and then use the new ball or color to complete the stitches.

However, some patterns require you to change in the middle of the row. To do this you must have around 36 inches of the original yarn left and work together the end of the remaining stitches using a double crochet until your original yarn runs out and then you use your new yarn as mentioned above.

To Fasten Off:

This involves removing the yarn from your crochet hook and is usually done at the end of the project or at the end of each separate section of the pattern. Making sure you fasten off ensures that your project and hard work will not unravel and you can do this by:

Cutting the yarn from the ball when you want to finish your project (ensuring you leave a 6 inch tail) and then using the hook to draw the tail through the last stitch and gently pulling tightly so that is does not undo.

Metric Conversions:

Crochet Hook & Knitting Needle Sizes			
U.S. Hook	U.S. Needle	Metric	U.K.
	0	2.00 mm	14
B-1	1	2.25 mm	13
C-2	2	2.75 mm	12
		3.00 mm	11
D-3	3	3.25 mm	10
E-4	4	3.50 mm	
F-5	5	3.75 mm	9
G-6	6	4.00 mm	8
7	7	4.50 mm	7
H-8	8	5.00 mm	6
I-9	9	5.50 mm	5
J-10	10	6.00 mm	4
K-10.5	10.5	6.50 mm	3
		7.00 mm	2
		7.50 mm	1
L	11	8.00 mm	0
M, N*	13	9.00 mm	00

N, P*	15	10.00 mm	000
P*		11.50 mm	
	17	13.00 mm	0000
	19	15.00 mm	00000
Q		15.75 mm	
S	35	19.00 mm	

*There are some differences between U.S. manufacturers on these sizes

Chapter 2 – Nautical Themed Cup Cozy

Perfect for the summer and an excellent way to add a nautical theme to the kitchen, these cup cozy's are cute and useful and you can also make matching coasters too! They are relatively easy to make and have wooden buttons to decorate to give it the finishing touch to keep your tea warm.

You Will Need

- Cotton Weight Yarn
- Crochet Hook Size G-6
- Needles and thread
- 2 Wooden Buttons

Pattern

Starting with a sl st on hook. Ch 16

Work 1st rw into back.

Round 1: 15 sc until end. Ch 1 and turn.

Round 2-15: 15 sc, ch 1 at end of each row. *Cut yarn and weave in the ends.*

Round 16: (using 2nd color) for the border. Start with sl st on hook and sc into one side of the square you have created.

Ch 1, sk a st, sc.

Repeat * to * around.

Round 17: When reaching a corner, sc, ch 1 and sc in same st. Ch 1, sk st, sc. Finish the rnd by sl st into 1st sc of rnd to join.

Round 18: (using new color) Make another rnd like 17, although sc into ch-1 sp into previous rnd. Calling this seed st.

Round 19-21: Repeat 2 rws of seed st. Finish last rw in the color as cozy center.

Round 22: Start with a sl st onto hook, ch 31. Work in the back of ch. 28 dc (3 extra ch for turning.)

Round 23: Ch 3 and turn. Dc into same st as ch 3. Dc until end of rw. 2 dc into last st (increase)

Round 24-28: repeat for 5 rws dc. Increase at beginning of each rw. Ch 3, dc into each st until end. (6 rws total)

Round 29: sc for border. 3 sc around dc for corners. 2 sc around each dc until corner. 3 sc, sc into V's until end.

Round 30: 2 sc around next dv, ch 20 (creating button loop). Sc into same sp for corner. 2 sc into next dc. For final row ch 17 to make 2nd button loop. 3 sc into corner and 1 sc into next st to finish border.

Round 31: (change yarn color) pull through loop between 1st and 2nd dc on top of rw. Putting hook between next 2 sts, pull a loop through onto hook. Sl st around next st until ending the rw.

Round 32-34: Repeat 2 striped making sl st

Round 35: sew on buttons by placing in the corner of the piece.

Round 36: weave in ends and fasten off. Neaten off the piece.

Chapter 3 – Lace Effect Mug Cozy

This pretty mug cozy is a versatile and adaptable pattern that you can adjust to fit any sized mug. With the lace effect it is a medium level difficulty but definitely worth the time and effort to create it. The wavy top edging also adds a dynamic layer to the piece that everyone can enjoy with their tea with an intricate handle cutout that looks professionally made.

You Will Need

- Worsted weight yarn
- Crochet Hook Size H-8
- Optional: button

Pattern Notes

- *Shell* (sh)– 3 treble (double crochet) chain 2, 3 treble (double crochet) into the same st.
- *Back post single crochet (Bpsc)* – worked around base of treble crochet st from the rw below, as follows: Right side facing you, insert hook from back-front on right side of st working around. Insert the hook into back of project on left side of st working around, YO, draw a loop up, YO, draw both loops through on the hook to finish stitch.

Pattern

Chain 4 and create a ring by joining with a slip stitch.

Rnd 1: chain 3, 11 double crochet into the ring and use a slip stitch to join in the 3rd chain at the start of the round. (st count 12)

Rond 2: chain 3, 1 double crochet into stitch at the base of chain-3, 2 treble crochet (double crochet) into each st until end and use a slip stitch to join in the 3rd chain at the start of the round. (st count 24)

Rnd 3: chain 3, double crochet into stitch at the base of chain-3, double crochet into next stitch,

2 double crochet into next stitch, 1 double crochet into next stitch

Repeat * to * until the end use a slip stitch to join in the 3rd chain at the start of the round. (st count 36)

Rnd 4: chain 1 (don't count as a stitch),

back post single crochet around double crochet in prev rnd

Repeat * to * until end and use a slip stitch into 1st chain 1 at the beginning of the round (stitch count 36)

Rnd 5: Chain 3, skip 2 stitches, sh into next stitch

sk 2 stitches, 1 double crochet into next 2 stitches, sk 2 stitches, sh into next st

Repeat * to * until you are left with 4 stitches and then sk 3 stitches, double crochet into last stitch and use a slip stitch into 3rd chain at the beginning of the rnd.

Rnd 6: Chain 3, sh in chain-2 sp of sh in prev rnd,

1 double crochet into next 2 double crochet from prev rnd, sh in chain-2 sp of sh from prev rnd

Repeat * to * X 3 (more), 1 double crochet into last stitch (this last st is 3rd chain from beginning of the prev rnd) don't join just turn (this allows a hole for the mug handle)

Rnd 7-end: Repeat rnd 6 until you reach the desired height (make sure this is at least ½ inch from the top of the rim to allow space to drink from the mug).

To finish

Once you have the correct height, don't cut the yarn, make a button loop by; chain 12, slip stitch into 1st of chain 12, single crochet around handle opening. Cut the yarn and fasten it off, leaving a tail to attach the button opposite the created button opening. Weave in ends.

Chapter 4 – Beginner Basic Coffee Sleeve

If you are new to making a cozy or are a beginner at crochet this is the perfect pattern because it is incredibly simple with fantastic results. You can interchange colors with this pattern or go for an easy solid block to start. This is a great foundation pattern that you can start with and adapt into something more intricate as you progress but in the meantime is excellent for protecting your hands against your hot coffee!

<u>You Will Need</u>

- Crochet Hook Size K
- Worsted Weight Yarn

<u>Pattern</u>

Rw 1: **Chain** 22, without twisting, slip stitch into the 1st chain to create a loop.

Rw 2: Chain 1, half double crochet into each chain around and use a slip stitch into the beginning chain-1 space to join. (st count 22 half double crochets)

Rw 3: Chain 1 and turn (this helps to make it look more even and natural), half double crochet into each half double crochet around and use a slip stitch into the beginning chain-1 space (stitch count 22 half double crochets)

Rws 4 - 6: Repeat rw 3 and fasten off to complete.

Chapter 5 – TMNT Cup Cozy

This cozy is perfect for a mug of kid's hot chocolate or other warm drinks and is a fun and unique way of protecting their hands from burning. Adding this unique twist is an interesting way of bringing crochet to a more modern setting and making it appeal to all ages. You can also give these as gifts or in party bags as an inexpensive creation that you can adapt to incorporate all of the teenage mutant ninja turtles by changing the band color.

<u>You Will Need</u>

- Worsted Weight yarn; orange, green, black and white.
- Crochet Hook G (for main cozy and eyes)
- Crochet Hook E for the pupils
- Needle

<u>Pattern Notes</u>

Half double crochet decrease (hdcdec): yarn over, insert the hook into next stitch, yarn over and pull a loop up, yarn over, insert the hook into the next stitch, yarn over and pull a loop up, yarn over, pull all 5 loops through on the hook.

<u>Pattern</u>

For the base:

Work continuously in rounds.

Round 1: (Using green and G crochet hook), chain 2, 6 single crochet into 2nd chain from the hook (6 single crochet)

Round 2: 2 single crochet into each single crochet around (12 single crochet)

Round 3: *2 single crochet into next stitch, single crochet* X 6 (18 single crochet)

Round 4: *2 single crochet into next stitch, 2 single crochet* X 6 (24 single crochet)

Round 5: *2 single crochet into next stitch, 3 single crochet* X 6 (30 single crochet)

Round 6: *2 single crochet into next stitch, 4 single crochet* X 6 (36 single crochet)

Round 7: *2 single crochet into next stitch, 5 single crochet* X 6 (42 single crochet)

<u>For the Sides:</u>

Work in rows backwards and forth

Row 8: chain 1 (not counted as st or throughout), only in the back loops half double crochet into each stitch around. Sl st into 1st half double crochet and turn. (42 half double crochet)

Row 9: Work in both the loops, half double crochet into each stitch around. Sl st into 1st half double crochet, chain 1 and turn (42 half double crochet)

Row 10: hdcdec across the next 2 stitches, 38 half double crochet, half double crochet decrease over the last 2 stitches, chain 1 and turn. Don't join. (40 half double crochet)

Row 11: half double crochet decrease over the next 2 stitches, 36 half double crochet, hdcdec over the last 2 stitches, chain 1 and turn (38 half double crochet)

Row 12: half double crochet into each stitch around and finish it off (cut the yarn). (38 half double crochet)

Row 13: (Using orange and join it with a sl st), chain 1, half double crochet into each stitch across, chain 1 and turn (38 half double crochet)

Row 14: half double crochet into each stitch around, chain 1 and turn (38 half double crochet)

Row 15: half double crochet into each stitch around and fasten off (cut the yarn) (39 half double crochet)

Row 16: (Using green and join it with a sl st) chain 1, half double crochet into each stitch around and fasten it off (cut the yarn) (38 half double crochet)

For the Ties:

Using the size G crochet hook, use a slip stitch to join the orange at the end of row 14, chain 30, single crochet into 2nd chain from the hook and into the next 3 stitches, half double crochet until the end of the chain, sl st until the end of row 15 and cut orange. (4 single crochet, 25 half double crochet)

Repeat again for the second side.

For the Eyes:

Round 1: (Using white and size G hook) chain 2, 6 single crochet into 2nd chain from the hook. Don't join (6 single crochet)

Round 2: 2 single crochet into each stitch around and sl st into 1st stitch (cut the white) (12 single crochet)

Round 3: (using orange, join using a single crochet into any stitch) single crochet into each stitch around, sl st into 1st stitch. Leave a longer tail and cut.

For the Pupils:

Row 1: (Using black and size E hook) chain 2, 6 single crochet into 2nd chain from the hook, sl st into 1st single crochet and leave a longer tail and cut. (6 single crochet)

To Assemble:

Using the black longer tail, sew the pupils on the eyes.

Fold it in half and place an eye either side of the fold, sewing them on using the orange long tail. Neaten it up and weave in the ends.

Chapter 6 – Rainbow Coffee Sleeve

A multi-colored cozy for any occasion that will bring a splash of color to your mornings. This easy to medium level project is a perfect follow on from the beginner cozy in chapter 4 because it is a fairly simple design but incorporates joining a lot of colors which can be trickier. This is a cup cozy that everyone can enjoy!

You Will Need

- Crochet Hook G-6
- Worsted Weight Yarn

Pattern Notes

- *Back post half double crochet (BPhdc);* YO, bring hook in back of st, insert hook right-left around st: YO, pull a loop up, YO again, pull the 3 loops onto hook.

Pattern

(Using red) create sl knot on the hook, chain 35. Using a sl st, join into 1st ch making sure to not twist ch.

Round 1: Ch 2, 1 half double crochet into each st. Use a sl st to join into 2nd ch of beginning ch-2

Round 2: half double crochet st around.

Round 3: (Using orange) ch 2. 1 back post half double crochet around each st.

Round 4: half double crochet all around.

Round 5: (using yellow) ch 2, 1 BPhdc into each st around.

Round 6: half double crochet all around.

Round 7: (Using green) ch 2, 1 BPhdc into each st around.

Round 8: half double crochet all around.

Round 9: (Using Blue) ch 2, 1 BPhdc into each st around.

Round 10: half double crochet all around.

Round 11: (Using Indigo) ch 2, 1 BPhdc into each st around.

Round 12: half double crochet all around.

Round 13: (Using Purple) ch 2, 1 BPhdc into each st around.

Round 14: half double crochet all around.

Fasten off and weave in ends.

Chapter 7 – Octopus Tea Sleeve Cozy

Fun and perfect for the big kids in the family, these grumpy octopi are cute for showing how we all feel before our morning coffee. Give these as gifts or take them into work as a conversation starter for a morning meeting as you are bound to get a few comments on these!

You Will Need

- Crochet Hook Size H-8
- Worsted Weight Yarn

Pattern Notes

- *Invisible decrease (invdec):* Put the hook into the front hook of the next stitch, in next st only put hook into front loop, yarn over and pull both loops through.
- This pattern works from top-bottom.
- Right side = outside, showing side.

Pattern

For the Body:

(using main color) Chain 38, slip stitch into 1st chain to create a ring (ensure there're no twists in the yarn here).

Round 1: Chain 1, 1 single crochet into each chain. Slip stitch into 1st single crochet to join (stitch count 38)

Rounds 2-3: Chain 1, single crochet around. Slip stitch into 1st single crochet to join. (St count 38)

Round 4: Chain 1. (invdec, 1 single crochet into next 17 stitches) X 2. Use a slip stitch to join into 1st single crochet (Stitch count 36)

Rounds 5-6: Chain 1 and single crochet around evenly. Use a slip stitch to join to 1st single crochet (stitch count 36)

Round 7: Chain 1. (invdec, 1 single crochet into next 16 stitches) X 2. Use a slip stitch to join to 1st single crochet (stitch count 34)

Rounds 8-9: Chain 1 and single crochet around evenly. Use a slip stitch to join to 1st single crochet (stitch count 34)

Round 10: Chain 1. (invdec, 1 single crochet into next 15 stitches) X 2. Use a slip stitch to join to 1st single crochet (stitch count 32)

Round 11: Chain 1 and single crochet around evenly. Use a slip stitch to join to 1st single crochet (stitch count 32)

Round 12: Chain 1.

Adding the legs - *1 single crochet into next 3 stitches, chain 13, skip 1st chain, and along 12 chains left, (2 single crochet into next chain, 1 single crochet into next chain) X 6. Slip stitch into next stitch*

Repeat * to * X 8. Use slip stitch to join into 1st single crochet. Fasten off and weave in ends.

<u>For the Eyes (Create 2 of these)</u>

(Using White)- With 8" create a magic ring

Round 1: 6 single crochet into the ring but don't join.

Round 2: *2 single crochet into next stitch, 1 single crochet into next stitch* X 3

Round 3: 1 single crochet into next 9 stitches. Slip stitch into next single crochet to join together. Fasten off and leave 12" tail to help sew.

<u>For the Eyelids (Also create 2)</u>

Using the main color – make a magic ring

Rw 1: Chain 1 and 4 single crochet into the ring.

Row 2: Chain 1 and turn. 2 single crochet into each stitch.

Row 3: Chain 2 and turn. Single crochet across evenly. Fasten off allowing an 18" tail to sew and weave in other ends.

<u>To Assemble</u>

1. The R3 of eyeballs should be on outside of the piece. 8" of yarn should be used as stuffing and the 12" tail should be used to sew onto the body (as seen in the picture)

2. The eyelids should be sewn onto the eyeballs making sure they are straight across the top. Sew all around the edges.

3. For the pupils you can stitch black yarn onto the eyeballs or even use pieces of felt and glue them on.

Chapter 8 – Christmas Reindeer Cup Cozy

This fantastic stocking filler is an excellent way to show some Christmas cheer in an understated way around the office or at home. With the cute antlers and easy design it is adaptable for larger or smaller mugs so that you can make them for everyone in every size (you could even make the whole reindeer set!)

<u>You will need</u>

- Cotton Weight Yarn
- Size E crochet Hook

<u>Pattern</u>

<u>For the main body:</u>

Row 1: chain 44 (plus 1 chain to turn), turn.

Row 2: 44 half double crochet and use a slip stitch to join to the 1st half double crochet.

Row 3: sl st into next st, 42 half double crochet.

Rows 4-15: chain 1 and turn, 42 half double crochet. (to make this project larger, add some more rows here)

Row 16: chain 12 (for the button hole, for larger buttons you may need to chain more), turn, 42 half double crochet and fasten it off.

<u>For the Antlers:</u>

Larger piece (X 2):

start by creating a magic ring.

Row 1: 4 single crochet into the ring.

Row 2 – End: 4 single crochet into ring until your piece reaches around 4cm

Smaller piece (X 2):

start by creating a magic ring.

Row 1: 4 single crochet into the ring.

Row 2 – End: 4 single crochet into ring until your piece reaches around 4cm

Stuff both pieces with filling and sew them together to make the antlers (pictured)

For the Tail:

Create a simple pompom that is around 3cm diameter

To Assemble:

Sew the antlers onto the main body at the front (you may need to fasten some stitches into the middle to stop them from flopping over the top)

Sew a button onto the top part by the handle and opposite the hole you created.

Sew on the tail, making sure to do so a few rows from the bottom.

Optional: single crochet into a small magic ring to create a small nose and sew this onto the front between the antlers (pictured)

Chapter 9– Taking Care of your Projects

Yarn can be difficult to wash and maintain if not dealt with properly and this could destroy your project (and all your hard work). Follow specific instructions for the yarn that you purchase as many sensitive fibers come with their own instructions and details of how to deal with it. If not, generally speaking the best way is to hand wash yarn in warm water with mild detergent and this will get rid of everyday dirt and grime from the project. On the other hand, mug cozies have a tendency to get spilled tea or coffee on them and this usually entails a more thorough wash in a machine. If this is the case, here are some basic washing tips to preserve your projects:

- Soak as soon as you can after the stain (this is the key to removing coffee stains) Soak in warm water to loosen the stain before putting on a wash.

- Do not wring out or vigorously wash the yarn e.g. a high spin cycle on the washing machine.

- Try to use non-biological washing powder for more sensitive fabrics

- To dry – re-shape when wet and then hang if possible.

- Only use a small amount of fabric softener (if any)

- Do not tumble dry

- Wash below 40 degrees.

The key point to remember is to keep your yarn away from heat, tumble drying will shrink and burn the project and it will be ruined. Following these steps ensures your projects will last a long time and you will be able to enjoy and show them off fully.

Chapter 10 – Final Notes and Advice

Hopefully this eBook has given you all the tips and tricks you need to make some fantastic projects and wonderful cup cozies. As you can see the possibilities are limitless and you may find you want to experiment to create your own characters! Feel free to adapt the patterns to suit you and your own cups or mugs and change the colors or designs. Lastly don't forget to properly take care of your projects so that they last as long as possible for you to enjoy them.

Thanks for reading and happy crocheting.

Crochet Coasters

Introduction

Have you just started crochet and are looking for something new to try? Are you looking for cool and fun themed items for your collection? Then you are in the right place.

The following patterns cover a range of holidays and themes for a fun and interesting side to crochet that will be the talking point of the room. Show of your crochet skills with each of these projects and you can use them when the right event or season arises. The patterns range in difficulty for beginners and experts so that you can keep coming back to the book as you progress.

Good luck and happy crocheting.

Chapter 1 – Mug Coasters

You Will Need:

- Crochet Hook Size H
- Worsted Weight Yarn

Pattern:

Rw 1: Using Main Color, ch 7, single crochet into 2nd chain from the hook (and all of the way down), ch 1 and turn (st count 6 single crochet)

Rw 2: Single crochet into each st along, ch 1 and turn (st count 6 single crochet)

Rw 3: 2 Single crochet into 1st st, single crochet into next 4 sts, 2 single crochet into last stitch, ch 1 and turn (st count 8 single crochet)

Rw 4: Single crochet into each st along, ch 1 and turn (st count 8 single crochet)

Rw 5: 2 Single crochet into 1st st, single crochet into next 6 sts, 2 single crochet into last st, ch 1 and turn (st count 10 single crochet)

Rw 6: Single crochet into each st along, ch 1 and turn (st count 10 single crochet)

Rw 7: 2 Single crochet into 1st st, single crochet into next 8 sts, 2 single crochet into last st, ch 1 and turn (st count 12 single crochet)

Rw 8-12: Single crochet into each st along, ch 1 and turn (12 single crochet)

(At end of rw 12, ch 2)

Rw 13: Double crochet, half double crochet, single crochet into next 8 sts, half double crochet, double crochet

Note: Here, do not fasten off main color but drop it off and change to brown, ch 1 and turn.

Rw 14: Single crochet into 1st 2 sts, half double crochet, double crochet into next 6 sts, half double crochet, single crochet into last 2 sts, fasten the brown off.

Now pick back up the main yarn color and sl st along the top of the brown only in the back loops. Continue single crochet around the edge and join using a sl st into 1st sl st, ch 1 and turn.

Make 2 sl st, ch 8, skip 5 sts and use a sl st to join. Sl st into next st, ch 1 and turn. Single crochet, 12 half double crochet around ch 8 join using single crochet, sl st into next st and fasten it off, weaving in the ends.

Chapter 2 – Wheel Coasters

You Will Need:

- Worsted Weight Yarn
- Crochet Hook Size G

Pattern:

Ch 4. Use a sl st to join to the 1st ch. (creates magic ring)

Round 1: Ch 3. 2 dc into ring.

Round 2: Ch 1, 3 dc into ring.

Repeat until 4 X 3 dc

Round 3: Sl st into 3rd ch of rnd 2. Change yarn color

Round 4: 2 sc into same st, 3rd ch of rnd 2.

Round 5: 2 sc into top of all dc, 1 sc into every 3 dc opening. (st count 28 sc). Sl st into 1st sc.

Round 6: (Change yarn color) Ch 3. 1 dc into every st around. (st count 28 dc). Sl st into 3rd ch of previous round.

Round 7: (Change yarn color) 2 sc into every st around. Fasten it off and weave in the ends.

Chapter 3 – Seaside Shell Coasters

You Will Need:

- Stitch Markers
- Worsted Weight Yarn
- Crochet Hook Size H
- Yarn Needle

Pattern Notes:

- Work this pattern in continuous rnds (don't turn unless indicated)
- Sl st should not count in the st count.

Pattern:

Create Magic Ring.

Round 1 (Right side): 6 single crochet into 2nd chain from the hook into magic ring and pull closed. (this will be your right side)

Round 2: 2 half double crochet into each stitch (12 half double crochet)

Round 3: 2 double crochet into each stitch (24 double crochet)

Round 4. 2 double crochet into 1st st

double crochet into next stitch, 2 double crochet into next stitch

Repeat * to * X 11, double crochet into next stitch (36 double crochet)

Round 5: Turn and chain 3 (this counts as the 1st double crochet)

2 double crochet into the next stitch, double crochet into next 2 stitches

Repeat * to * X 3

2 half double crochet into next stitch, half double crochet into next 2 stitches

Repeat ** to ** Twice, 2 single crochet into next stitch, single crochet into next stitch, slip stitch into next stitch and fasten off (24 stitches)

For the Edges:

Round 6 (Right Side): With the right side facing you, Use a slip stitch to join the brown yarn into the same stitch that last stitch in rnd 4 was worked in. Slip stitch into each stitch around (but don't work into sides of sts on rnds 4-5) Fasten it off.

Using brown yarn, needle and running st (or backstitch) embroider spiral detailing. Starting at 1st st of the edge round and slowly working inwards on the natural spiral that is created. Don't embroider the sts under round 5! Work outwards again to add perpendicular linings making sure to naturally increase the gaps between as you are going along. Weave in the ends neatly.

Chapter 4 – Apple Fruit Bowl Coasters

You Will Need:

- Needle
- Worsted Weight Yarn
- Crochet Hook Size H

Pattern:

Using White Yarn, create a magic circle, ch 2, 12 double crochet inside circle and join it to the 1st double crochet, ch 2.

Rnd 2: 2 double crochet into each st around, join and ch 2 (24 double crochet)

Rnd 3: 2 double crochet into 1st st, double crochet into next st, repeat all the way around and join. (36 double crochet)

Changing to red, ch 1

Rnd 4: 2 single crochet into each st around, join and fasten it off, weave in all the ends (72 single crochet)

For the Leaf:

- *Crochet Hook Szie E*
- *Worsted Weight Yarn*

Chain 5,

Round 1 – single crochet into 2nd ch from the hook, half double crochet into next st, double crochet into next st, work (2 half double crochet into last, chain 2, single crochet into 2nd chain from the hook, 2 half double crochet) into the last chain.

Work on opposite side to your base chain, double crochet into next, half double crochet into next st and single crochet into the last.

Fasten it off using a slip stitch into the 1st single crochet of the round but leave a 6 inch tail to sew onto the apple.

For the Stem

Using brown – ch 7, double crochet into 2nd ch from the hook, single crochet the rest of the ch. Fasten it off allowing a long tail that can help you to sew to the top.

End with tying brown to create seeds inserting the hook into sl st, parallel and opposite each other on the 1st round (pictured)

Chapter 5 – Beginner Star Coasters

You Will Need:

- Crochet Hook Size H
- Cotton Weight Yarn

Pattern:

Round 1: Chain 4, work 9 double crochet into 4th chain from the hook and join into the top of the beginning chain 4 (10 double crochet)

Round 2: Chain 3, double crochet, chain 2, 2 double crochet into same stitch (this creates the beginning corner)

double crochet into the next stitch (2 double crochet, chain 2, 2 double crochet) into next stitch – corner created

Repeat * to * X 4. Double crochet into next stitch and join into the beginning chain 3 (25 double crochet) slip stitch into next stitch and chain2 space.

Round 3: Beginning Corner.

[*Double crochet into 2 stitches, Sip stitch into next stitch, double crochet into 2 stitches* corner into next chain 2 space] X 4

Repeat * to * once and join. (40 double crochet, 5 slip stitches). Slip stitch into next chain and chain 2 space.

Round 4: Chain 1, (3 single crochet) into the same space.

[*Single crochet into 4 stitches, slip stitch into slip stitch, single crochet into 4 stitches*. (3 single crochet) into next chain 2 space] X 4 Repeat * to * once and join into 1st single crochet. (55 single crochet, 5 slip stitch) Fasten Off.

Chapter 6 – Disney Coasters

You Will Need:

- Worsted Weight Yarn (black)
- Crochet Hook Size H

Pattern Notes:

- Chain 1 does not count as the 1st st

Pattern:

For the main body:

Chain 2, 8 single crochet into 2nd chain from the hook.

Round 1: Chain 1, 2 single crochet into each stitch around. Slip stitch into chain 1 sp to join. (st count 16)

Round 2: Chain 1,

single crochet into next stitch, 2 single crochet into following stitch

Repeat * to * X 7, Slip stitch into chain 1 sp to join. (st count 24)

Round 3: Chain 1,

single crochet into next 2 stitches, 2 single crochet into next stitch

Repeat * to * X 7. Slip stitch into chain 1 sp to join. (st count 32)

Round 4: Chain 1,

single crochet into next 3 stitches, 2 single crochet into next stitch

Repeat * to * X 7. Slip stitch into chain 1 sp to join. (st count 40)

Round 5: Chain 1, slip stitch into each stitch around. Slip stitch to chain 1 sp to join. (st count 40) Fasten off.

<u>For the Ears – Create Two</u>

Chain 2, 8 single crochet into 2nd chain from the hook

Round 1 - Chain 1, 2 single crochet into each stitch around and slip stitch into chain 1 sp to join. (st count 36)

Round 2 - Chain 1,

*Single crochet into next stitch, 2 single crochet into next stitch

Repeat * to * X 7 and slip stitch into chain 1 sp to join. (st count 24). Tie it off and leave a 6" tail.

Using the tails of the ears, sew them onto the top of the coaster slightly off-center but evenly. Weave in ends.

Chapter 7 – Cute Cake Coasters

You Will Need:

- Cotton Weight Yarn
- Size H-6 Crochet Hook
- Needle

Pattern:

Using Brown (CA) Chain 10

Round 1: Single crochet 8 and turn.

Round 2: chain 1, single crochet 8 into back sts

Round 3 – 14: Repeat rnds 1-2 12 times. (14 altogether)

Using Color B

Round 15: chain 1, single crochet 1 into sides of rw 14 (each) and turn. [leave CB attached and do not cut it] (Count 14)

Using color C

Round 16: chain 1, single crochet 2 into 1st stitch, single crochet 1 into next 12, single crochet 2 into next and turn (count 16)

Round 17: Do not chain, sk 1st stitch, single crochet into next 14 sts except one from the end and turn. (Count 14)

Round 18: chain 1, single crochet into each and turn (Count 14)

Round 19: Do not chain, sk 1st stitch, single crochet into next 12 sts except one from the end and turn. (Count 12)

Round 20: chain 1, single crochet into each and turn (Count 12)

Round 21: chain 1, single crochet into each and turn (Count 12)

Round 22: Do not chain, sk 1st stitch, single crochet into each and turn (Count 11)

Round 23: Do not chain, sk 1st stitch, single crochet into each and turn (Count 10)

Round 24: Do not chain, sk 1st stitch, single crochet into each and turn, cut off and tie ends (Count 9)

For the Cherry:

Count 3 sts in from the top and pull the 4th stitch from the end through on round 24.

Round 25: single crochet into the 4th st from the end and the next 2 and turn. (Count 3)

Round 26: Do not chain, sk 1st st, single crochet into next 2 and turn. (Count 2)

Round 27: Do not chain, sk 1st stitch, single crochet into the last stitch, cut the yarn and tie it off. (Count 1)

For the Edging

Round 28: (Using color B that you left on round 15). Pull through the end of round 15 and single crochet into each round and stitch all the way round the edging. Cut it and tie it off. (Count Approx. 59)

Chapter 8 – Umbrella Coasters

You Will Need:

- Cotton Weight Yarn
- Crochet Hooks Size E and G

Pattern Notes:

- Make sure to cut the yarn after each color change.

Pattern:

With 1 color: Chain 4, slip stitch into the 1st chain to create a magic ring.

Round 1: Chain 1. 7 double crochet into the ring. Slip stitch into the chain and pull through the red yarn. (8 stitches)

Round 2: Chain 1. [2 double crochet into the next stitch] X7. 1 double crochet. Slip stitch into chain. (16 stitches)

Round 3: Chain 1. 1 double crochet. [2 double crochet into the next stitch, 1 double crochet] X7, 1 double crochet, slip stitch to chain using main color. (24 stitches)

Round 4: Chain 1, 2 double crochet [2 double crochet into the next stitch, 2 double crochet] X7, 1 double crochet, slip stitch to the chain using the orange yarn (32 stitches)

Round 5: Chain 1, 3 double crochet. [2 double crochet into next stitch, 3 double crochet] X7, 1 double crochet, slip stitch to chain. (40 stitches)

Round 6: Chain 1, 4 double crochet. [2 double crochet into next stitch, 4 double crochet] X7, 1 double crochet, slip stitch to chain using the main color. (48 Stitches)

Round 7: Chain 1, 5 double crochet [2 double crochet into next stitch, 5 double crochet] X7, 1 double crochet, slip stitch to chain using the yellow yarn. (56 stitches)

Round 8: Chain 1, 6 double crochet. [2 double crochet into next stitch, 6 double crochet] X7, 1 double crochet, slip stitch to chain. (64 stitches)

Round 9: Chain 1, 7 double crochet. [2 double crochet into next stitch 7 double crochet] X7, 1 double crochet and slip stitch to the chain using main color. (72 Stitches)

Round 10: Chain 1, 8 double crochet. [2 double crochet into next stitch, 8 double crochet] X7, 1 double crochet and slip stitch to chain using green. (80 stitches)

Round 11: Chain 1, 9 double crochet. [2 double crochet into next stitch, 9 double crochet] X7, 1 double crochet and slip stitch to chain. (88 stitches)

Round 12: Chain 1, 10 double crochet. [2 double crochet into next stitch, 10 double crochet] X7, 1 double crochet and slip stitch to chain using main color. (96 stitches)

Round 13: Chain 1, 11 double crochet. [2 double crochet into next stitch, 11 double crochet] X7, 1 double crochet and slip stitch to chain using the blue yarn. (104 stitches)

Round 14: Chain 1, 12 double crochet. [2 double crochet into next stitch, 12 double crochet] X7, 1 double crochet and slip stitch to chain. (112 stitches)

Round 15: Chain 1, 13 double crochet. [2 double crochet into next stitch, 13 double crochet] X7, 1 double crochet and slip stitch to chain using main color (120 stitches)

Round 16: Chain 1, 14 double crochet. [2 double crochet into next stitch, 14 double crochet] X7, 1 double crochet and slip stitch to chain using the purple yarn. (128 stitches)

Round 17: Chain 1, 15 double crochet. [2 double crochet into next stitch, 15 double crochet] X7, 1 double crochet and slip stitch to chain. (136 stitches)

Round 18: Chain 1, 16 double crochet. [2 double crochet into next stitch, 16 double crochet] X7, 1 double crochet and slip stitch to chain using the main color. (144 stitches)

Round 19: Chain 1, 17 double crochet. [2 double crochet into next stitch, 17 double crochet] X7, 1 double crochet and slip stitch to chain. (152 stitches)

Cut the yarn and weave in all the ends.

Chapter 9 – Superbowl Coasters

You Will Need:

- Needle
- Crochet Hook Size H-8
- Worsted Weight Yarn

Pattern Notes:

- Beginning Chain 2 doesn't count as a stitch.
- To keep even edges turn your piece anti-clockwise

Pattern:

For the body:

Round 1: Chain 2, 2 half double crochet in 2nd chain from the hook, chain 2 and turn. (Count 2)

Round 2: 2 half double crochet into each stitch, chain 2 and turn. (Count 4)

Round 3: half double crochet, 2 half double crochet into next 2 stitches, half double crochet, chain 2 and turn. (Count 6)

Round 4: half double crochet, 2 half double crochet, half double crochet into next 2 stitches, half double crochet, chain 2 and turn. (Count 8)

Round 5: half double crochet, 2 half double crochet into next stitch, half double crochet into next 4 stitches, 2 half double crochet into next stitch, half double crochet, chain 2 and turn. (Count 10)

Round 6: half double crochet, 2 half double crochet into next stitch, half double crochet into next 6 stitches, 2 half double crochet into next stitch, half double crochet, chain 2 and turn. (Count 12)

Rounds 7-10: half double crochet into each stitch along, chain 2 and turn. (Count 12)

Round 11: half double crochet, hdc2tog, half double crochet into next 6 stitches, hdc2tog, half double crochet, chain 2 and turn. (Count 10)

Round 12: half double crochet, hdc2tog, half double crochet into next 4 stitches, hdc2tog, half double crochet, chain 2 and turn. (Count 8)

Round 13: half double crochet, hdc2tog, half double crochet into next 2 stitches, hdc2tog, half double crochet, chain 2 and turn. (Count 6)

Round 14: half double crochet, hdc2tog X2, half double crochet, chain 2 and turn. (Count 4)

Round 15: hdc2tog X 2, chain 2 and turn. (Count 2)

Round 16: hdc2tog X 1, chain 1 and turn. (Count 1)

Round 17: single crochet around (evenly) and fasten off, weaving in all the ends.

<u>For the detailing:</u>

Using the white yarn, stitch on the top between round 4 and 5. Weave the tails on the wrong side. Then use the white yarn to stitch on the top between rows 12 and 13 (again weaving the tails on the wrong side)

With 2 strands white, using tapestry needle use straight stitches to embroider your coaster with laces. Secure ends to WS of coaster.

Chapter 10 – Orange & Lemon Coasters

You Will Need:

- Worsted Weight Yarn
- Crochet Hook Size H
- Needle

Pattern:

Using white yarn to start, create a magic circle, ch 1, 12 single crochet inside the circle, join to the 1st single crochet and then change to the main color of your fruit, ch 2 (12 single crochet)

Rnd 2: 2 double crochet into each st around, join and ch 2 (24 double crochet)

Rnd 3: 2 double crochet into 1st st, double crochet into next st, repeat all the way around and join. Change back to white yarn, ch 1 (36 double crochet)

Rnd 4: 2 single crochet into 1st st, single crochet into next 2 sts, repeat all the way around and change yarn color back to main, ch 1 (48 single crochet)

Rnd 5: Single crochet into each st around and join it to the 1st single crochet, fasten off and weave in all ends. (48 single crochet)

For the segments:

Use surface slip stitching to create the different sections using the white yarn. There should be 6 in total and shoot them out from every other st in rnd 1. Weave in all the ends.

Chapter 11 – Contrast Swirl Coasters

You Will Need:

- Crochet Hook Size G-6
- Light Weight Yarn

Pattern Notes:

- Worked in continuous rounds, don't join at the end of rnds.

Pattern:

Using Color A, Create a magic circle.

Rnd 1: Chain 1 (Not counted as stitch (here or throughout), 6 single crochet into the circle (6 stitches).

Rnd 2: 2 single crochet into each stitch around. (12 stitches)

Rnd 3: *2 single crochet into next stitch, 1 single crochet into next stitch, 1 single crochet into next stitch*

Repeat * to * around. (18 stitches).

Rnd 4: *2 single crochet into next stitch, 1 single crochet into each of next 2 stitches*

Repeat * to * around. (24 stitches)

Rnd 5: *2 single crochet into next stitch, 1 single crochet into each of next 3 stitches*

Repeat * to * around. (30 stitches)

Rnd 6: *2 single crochet into next stitch, 1 single crochet into each of next 4 stitches*

Repeat * to * around. (36 stitches)

Rnd 7: *2 single crochet into next stitch, 1 single crochet into each of next 5 stitches*

Repeat * to * around. (42 stitches)

Rnd 8: *2 single crochet into next stitch, 1 single crochet into each of next 6 stitches*

Repeat * to * around. (48 stitches)

Rnd 9: *2 single crochet into next stitch, 1 single crochet into each of next 7 stitches*

Repeat * to * around. (54 stitches)

Slip stitch into next 2 stitches and fasten it off.

Using color B – work only on the surface sts to create the spiral. Keep the yarn you are working on the back of the project, add the hook front to back at the 1st st from rnd 1 (in the top) and pull up a loop of the yarn.

Add the hook front to back through the next stitch, pick the yarn up and pull the loop on the hook (creates 1 surface st)

Repeat * to * until you have created the pattern all around, fasten it off and weave in all the ends.

Chapter 12 – Spring Flower Coasters

<u>You Will Need:</u>

- Cotton Weight Yarn
- Crochet Hook Size F
- Needle
- Stitch Markers

<u>Pattern Notes:</u>

- The flower center is crocheted in rounds without joining the ends.

<u>Pattern:</u>

Rnd 1: (Using Yellow) Chain 2, 6 single crochet into 2nd chain from the hook, don't join the rnd. (6 single crochet)

Rnd 2: 2 single crochet into each stitch around, don't join the rnd. (12 single crochet)

Rnd 3: *2 single crochet into next stitch, single crochet into next stitch*

Repeat * to * around but don't join the rnd. (18 single crochet)

Rnd 4: *2 single crochet into next stitch, single crochet into next 2 stitches*

Repeat * to * around and use a slip stitch to join to the beginning single crochet. Fasten off the yellow (24 single crochet)

Rnd 5: (Using white) Use a slip stitch to join into any stitch, chain 1, single crochet into same stitch as the one that was joined. Into the next stitch, work:

(single crochet, chain 5, single crochet into 4th chain from the hook and single crochet into the last chain, single crochet into same stitch as 1st single crochet) – this creates the first point. Single crochet into next stitch, chain 1,

single crochet into next stitch, in next stitch work: (single crochet, chain 5, single crochet into 4th chain from the hook and single crochet into last chain, then single crochet into same stitch as the 1st single crochet), single crochet into next stitch, chain 1

Repeat * to * around and use a slip stitch to join to the beginning single crochet. (32 single crochet around – don't include the points, 8 chain-1 sps, 8 points)

For the Petals:

Rnd 6: Skip the 1st 2 single crochet stitches, work along the right-hand side of the 1st point. (half double crochet, double crochet) into 1st stitch, 2 double crochet into next stitch, 4 double crochet into sp at top of tip. Work down left-hand side of tip, 2 double crochet into next stitch, (double crochet, half double crochet) into last stitch, sk next 2 single crochet stitches on rnd, slip stitch into chain-1 sp.

skip the next 2 single crochet stitches, work up right-hand side of next point, (half double crochet, double crochet) into 1st stitch, 2 double crochet into next stitch, 4 double crochet into sp at top of tip, work down left-hand side of tip, 2 double crochet into next stitch (double crochet, half double crochet) into last stitch, sk next 2 single crochet stitches on rnd, slip stitch into chain-1 sp

Repeat * to * all around. Fasten off and weave in all the ends.

Chapter 13 – Valentine's Day Coasters

You Will Need:

- Worsted Weight Yarn
- Crochet Hook Size F

Pattern:

Chain 8, slip stitch into 1st chain to create a ring.

Rnd 1: Chain 2 (count this as 1st double crochet) 16 double crochet into the ring, slip stitch into top of the chain 2 to join. (17 double crochet)

Rnd 2: Chain 1 and turn (single crochet chain 2) into the same double crochet, (half double crochet, chain 1) into next 2 stitches, (single crochet, chain 1) into next 5 stitches, (single crochet, chain 1 X 2) into next stitch, (single crochet, chain 1) into next 5 stitches, (half double crochet, chain 1) into next 3 stitches but don't join here.

Rnd 3: Turn, (single crochet, chain 1) into the next chain space, (half double crochet, chain 1) into next chain sp, (double crochet, chain 1) into next 2 chain spaces, (half double crochet, chain 1) into next 4 chain spaces, (double crochet, chain 1 X 2) into next chain space, (half double crochet, chain 1) into next 4 chain spaces, (double crochet, chain 1) into next 2 chain spaces, (half double crochet, chain 1) into next space, single crochet into last chain space and slip stitch into the top of (single crochet, chain 1), chain 2, single crochet in the space between the top 2 double crochet of the 1st rnd, chain 1, slip stitch into the 1st chain 1.

Rnd 4 –Don't turn, chain 4, half double crochet into chain-space, (chain 3, hdc) into the next 2 chain spaces, (chain 3, sc) into the next 5 chain spaces,

For the picot at the bottom point – (chain 4, single crochet into 3rd chain from the hook, chain 1) sk next 2 double crochet, (single crochet, chain 3) into next 5 chain spaces, (half double crochet, chain 3) into next 2 chain spaces, (half double crochet, chain 4) into single crochet, slip stitch between the 2 double crochets of the 1st rnd, chain 3, slip stitch into the base of 1st chain-4 space.

Rnd 5 – Don't turn, chain 3, (single crochet, chain 3 twice) into next chain 4 space, (single crochet, chain 3) into next 7 chain 3 spaces, (single crochet, chain 3 twice) into picot center, (single crochet, chain 3) into next 7 chain 3 spaces, (single crochet, chain 3 twice) into the last chain space, slip stitch into slip stitch and slip stitch into the 1st chain coming out of slip stitch to finish it off. Fasten off and weave in all the ends

Chapter 14 – Snowflake Winter Coasters

You Will Need:

- Crochet Hook Size G
- Cotton Weight Yarn
- Needle

Pattern Notes:

- Expert Pattern – Uses the picot stitch
- Work in the round

Pattern:

Rw 1 (using color A): Make a magic ring, chain 1, single crochet X 6 into the ring, sl stitch into 1st stitch to join. (6 single crochet)

Rw 2: Chain 5 (count as double crochet + chain 2),

double crochet into next stitch, chain 2

Repeat * to * X 4 (more), use a sl stitch into the stitch. (6 double crochet)

Rw 3: Chain 1, single crochet into same stitch to join,

[half double crochet, double crochet, chain 2, double crochet, half double crochet] into next chain 2 sp,

*single crochet into next stitch, [half double crochet, double crochet, chain 2, double crochet, half double crochet] into next chain 2 sp.

Repeat * to * X 4 (more), sl stitch into 1st stitch securing (6 single crochet, 12 half double crochet, 12 double crochet)

Fasten this color off.

Rw 4 (Using color B): Sl st into chain0-2 sp, chain 1, single crochet into same stitch, chain 6,

single crochet into next chain-2 sp, chain 6

Repeat * to * X 4 (more) and sl stitch into 1st single crochet securing it. (6 single crochet)

Rw 5: Chain 1,

single crochet into same stitch as the join, [half double crochet, 4 double crochet, chain 4, 4 double crochet, half double crochet] into next chain-6 sp

Repeat * to * X 4 (more), sl stitch into 1st single crochet securing it. (6 single crochet, 12 half double crochet, 48 double crochet)

Fasten this color off.

Rw 6 (using color A): Sk joining st, sk next half double crochet, sk next double crochet, sl st into next stitch, chain 1, single crochet into same stitch you sl st into, single crochet into next 2 stitches, [2 single crochet, picot, 2 single crochet] into next chain-4 sp, single crochet into next 3 stitches, chain 5, sk next double crochet and half double crochet and single crochet and half double crochet and double crochet,

single crochet into next 3 stitches, [2 single crochet, picot, 2 single crochet] into next chain-4 sp, single crochet into next 3 stitches, chain 5, sk next double crochet and half double crochet and single crochet and half double crochet and double crochet

Repeat * to * X 4 (more) and sl st into 1st single crochet securing it. (60 single crochet)

Fasten it off.

Chapter 15 – Pear Fruit Bowl Coasters

You Will Need:

- Worsted Weight Yarn
- Crochet Hook Size H
- Needle

Pattern:

Using White yarn, create a magic ring, ch 2, 12 double crochet inside ring and join to 1st double crochet, ch 2.

Rnd 2: 2 double crochet into each st around, join and ch 2 (st count 24 double crochet)

Rnd 3: 2 double crochet into 1st st, double crochet into next st, repeat all the way around, join and ch 1 (st count 36 double crochet)

Rw 4: single crochet into next 8 sts, ch 1 and turn.

Rw 5: Single crochet dec, single crochet into next 4 sts, single crochet dec, ch1 and turn.

Rw 6: Single crochet along (6 single crochet)

Rw 7: Single crochet dec, single crochet into next 2 sts, single crochet dec, ch1 and turn.

Rw 8: Create 2 single crochet decs, ch 1,

Using Green, single crochet around the entire edge and join to the 1st single crochet. Fasten it off and weave in all the ends.

For the Stem

Using brown – ch 7, double crochet into 2nd ch from the hook, single crochet the rest of the ch. Fasten it off allowing a long tail that can help you to sew to the top.

End with tying brown to create seeds, parallel opposite each other on the 1st round (pictured)

Chapter 16 – Final Notes and Advice

Hopefully this eBook has given you some interesting and challenging new projects to add to your crochet collection. Feel free to adjust or adapt the pattern colors to suit your own needs and color scheme within your house. You could even give some of these as gifts near the holidays or as party favors for themed events, the possibilities are limitless.

For these coaster projects, try to avoid washing them on high settings and settle for a warm hand wash or a low machine wash. Avoid tumble drying and bleach altogether as this can ruin the yarn and shrink your patterns. In addition to this, if you drop tea or coffee (or wine) on them, soak them immediately for a better chance to remove the stain from the material. Taking care of your projects is the key to them lasting for many years to come.

If you found you struggled with some of these projects, do not feel disheartened as some are a higher difficulty than others. Try a simpler project before attempting it again to hone your crochet skills as practice makes perfect.

Thank you for reading.

Crochet Baby Dress Patterns

Introduction

Each dress you create from this book will have everyone commenting on your crochet skills because these dresses are just too darn cute! Before you choose your first dress project, you may need a few pointers on choosing yarns. All yarn is not the same, some are thicker, some are softer, some are wool, some are not…you get the picture.

Choosing yarn for a baby dress is not a difficult task. The yarn type is listed on the pattern; if it says use sport or baby then this would be the best yarn for the project, but, always read the label on the package. The label will specify the washing instructions and this is the most important part of choosing yarn for baby. The label will give washing instructions/care instructions and also tell you what kind of fibers are used; acrylic, cotton, wool, and wool blend are a few of the types of yarn available.

If you are going to decorate the dress with any fancy stitches or trim, you may want to have a look at specialty yarns. These yarns come in many different textures and fibers. Specialty yarn can dress up a cute pattern and personalize it. You may want to have a look at specialty yarns if you plan to make any appliques. Remember to check the label and choose yarn that is washable and easy to care for.

Another tip for choosing yarn is…. softness! The softness of the yarn is important for keeping baby comfortable; remember those itchy hats, sweaters, or mittens you hated as a child? Feeling the yarn against the back of your hand, or inner arm will give you an idea of the texture and how it will feel against her soft skin. That's about it on yarn, color is all about your taste and style.

Before digging in and starting that adorable dress, take a moment to learn how to decrease and increase when crocheting. If you already know, great! But if you are new to crochet, it is a good idea to take a moment and learn how to increase and decrease. Increasing will allow you to make the garment wider/bigger and decrease will allow you to make the garment narrower/smaller. This skill is not hard to learn, there are a multitude of videos available on the internet that will show you exactly how to add this skill to your crochet repertoire.

If you are new to crochet, don't panic, these patterns are easy to use and the stitches are basic. If this is your first big crochet project, it may be a good idea to check out the appliques. The bonus appliques included in this book use basic stitches, they are great for practicing.

Ok, so now you have the perfect yarn, you are up to speed on the stitches, you have learned to decrease and increase, now it's time to make that beautiful dress for the little princess in your life. If you have any problems reading the patterns, remember there is a crochet stitch chart to help you out.

Chapter 1 – Guide for Crochet Terms and Hooks

Before you begin, look over this chapter to familiarize yourself with the abbreviations used in this book. The abbreviations are standard crochet terms, if you do not know the stitches covered in the abbreviations, it is easy to find an online tutorial for beginners.

If you are already familiar with the stitches listed in the abbreviation chart, you will have no problem crocheting the patterns in this book. The patterns for each project use these abbreviations and hook sizes. If you are unfamiliar with these abbreviations, there are many good crochet stitch tutorials online to help you.

Crochet Abbreviations

beg – Beginning	bg - Block
cc – Contrast Color	ch – chain
dc – Double Crochet	dec – Decrease
dtr – Double Treble Crochet	hdc – Half Double Crochet
htr – Half Treble Crochet	inc – Increase
rep – Repeat	rnd – Round
sc – Single Crochet	sl st – Slip Stitch

sp(s) – Space(s)	st(s) – Stitch(s)
tog – Together	tr – Treble Crochet
tr tr – Treble Treble Crochet	WS – Wrong Side
yo – Yarn Over	RS – Right Side
( ) – Work instructions within the parentheses as many times as directed	* - Repeat instructions following the single asterisk as directed
** - Repeat the instructions within the asterisk as many times as directed	[ ] – Work instructions within the brackets as many times as instructed

Crochet Hook Sizes

U.S.	English	Metric
14	6	0.60
12	5	0.75
10	4	1.00
-	3	1.25
6	2.5	1.50

4	2	1.75
B	14	2.00
C	12	2.50
D	11	3.00
E	9	3.50
F	8	4.00
G	7	4.50
H	6	5.00
I	5	5.50
J	4	6.00
K	2	7.00
-	1/0	8.00
-	2/0	9.00
P	3/0	10.00

Chapter 2 – Pink Summer Sun Dress

Size: 12 month

Skill Level: Beginner-Intermediate

Materials: 5mm crochet hook, 1 skein of sport weight yarn in main color and 1 skein of contrast color.

Note for Special Stitches:

Scallop- 2dc, 1ch, 2dc, all in the same st

Shell- 5dc all in the same st

Cluster- *YO, insert hook into the st indicated then YO and draw up a loop* repeat *to* 4 times now YO and draw through all 9 loops on the hook then Ch1 to secure cluster.

Beginning Cluster- Pull up a loop and *YO then insert the hook into the st indicated now YO and draw up a loop* repeat *to* 3 times, now YO and draw through all 9 loops on the hook then Ch1 to secure cluster.

Pattern

Yoke

Ch61

Row 1: Hdc in the 3rd ch from the hook and in the next 5 sts, hdc 3 in the next st, *hdc in the next 14 sts then hdc 3 in the next st* now rep from *to* 2 more times then hdc in the last 7 sts and turn

Row 2: Ch 2 (this counts as the 1st hdc) then hdc in each st across now work 3 hdc in the centre st of each 3-hdc corner group and turn

Rows 3-7: Repeat Row 2

Row 8: Join with a sl st and work the same as Row 2 but in the round

Row 9: Change to CC yarn and work a beginning cluster in the first st then *sk the next st and cluster in the next st* now repeat * to* in the round then join to the first cluster with a sl st and Do Not Turn

Row 10: (the armholes) Change to MC yarn and ch 2 then hdc in each sp and cluster across to the first corner then sk the next clusters to the second corner and hdc in the next cluster now continue hdc across in each sp and cluster to the third corner and sk the next clusters to the fourth corner and hdc in the next corner and continue across back.

Skirt

Row 1: Ch 3 (this counts as the 1st dc) then [1dc, 1ch, 2dc] in the same st and sk the next st then *scallop in the next st and sk the next st* now repeat *to* in the round and join to the first dc with a sl st.

Rd 2: Sl st across to the 1st ch and sp then ch 3 and [1dc, 1ch, 2dc] in the same st now scallop in each remaining scallop around and join to the first dc with a sl st.

Rows 3-20: Repeat Rd 2.

Row 21: Change to CC yarn and sl st across to the 1st ch and sp now ch 3 then dc 4 in the same st now shell in each remaining scallop around and join with a sl st to the first dc and fasten off

Neck

Join CC yarn to the bottom of the opening at the back of the yoke. Ch 1 and sc evenly up the right side. At the top of the side [1sc, 1ch, 1sc] in the top st and continue with sc evenly around the neck and down the other side of the back opening. Attach a button on the opposite side of the ch sp for fastening.

Cluster Stitch Layered Flower

Bottom Layer- Use CC and make a Magic Ring for 5 sc and sl st to join the round. *[Ch 3, Cluster st, ch 3, sl st] into the same st then sl st into the next st* and repeat *to* around. Fasten off and leave a medium length tail.

Top Layer- Use CC and make a Magic Ring for 5 sc. Sl st to join the round. Change to MC and (Turn the flower to the opposite side) now *[Ch 3, Cluster st, ch 3, sl st] into the same st and sl st into the next st* then repeat *to* around and fasten off leaving a long tail.

Sew Top Layer onto the Bottom Layer this makes the petals of the Bottom Layer show between the petals of the Top Layer then attach to dress flower to the shoulder of the dress as in the picture.

Chapter 3 – Blue Angel Pinafore

Size: 0-3 months

Skill Level: Beginner-intermediate

Materials: Size H hook, 1-2 skeins of sport weight yarn in a soft blue. (you can choose any color you like) 2 small, cute buttons

Pattern

ch 52

Row 1:   Sc in the 2nd ch from the hook and in each ch across

Row 2:   ch 3 and turn the project then dc in the next 2 sts. * dc 2 in the next st and dc in the next 3 sts* and repeat from *to* 11 times now dc in the remaining sts to the end

Row 3:   ch 3 and turn the project then dc in the next 3 sts. *dc 2 in the next st and dc in the next 4 sts* repeat *to* 11 times and dc in the remaining st then dc on top of the ch 3

Row 4:   ch 3 and turn the project then dc in the next 3 sts, now *dc 2 in the next st and dc in the next 4 sts* repeat *to* 13 times and dc in the remaining sts then dc on top of the ch 3

Row 5:   ch 3 and turn the project then dc in the same st. Now *skip the next st then shell (shell-2dc ch 2 2dc) in the next st* and repeat *to* to the end and dc 2 on top of the ch 3

Row 6:   ch 3 and turn then dc in the same st and shell in the next 6 shells then ch 3 and skip the next 10 shells. Shell in the next 11 shells then ch 3 and skip the next 10 shells now shell in the next 6 shells and dc 2 on the top of the ch 3

Row 7: ch 3 and turn then dc in the same st. Shell in the next 6 shells and dc in the next 3 ch then shell in the next 11 shells. Now dc in each of the 3 ch and shell in the next 6 shells then 2dc on top of the ch 3

Row 8: ch 3 and turn then dc in the same st. Shell in the next 6 shells then skip the first dc of the underarm and shell in the next dc. Shell in the next 11 shells and skip the first dc of the underarm and shell in the next dc. Shell in the next 6 shells and dc 2 on top of the ch 3

Row 9: ch 3 and turn then dc in the same st. Shell in each shell to the end and dc 2 on top of the ch 3

Rows 10-17: Repeat row 9

Row 18: ch 3 and turn then dc in the same st. Sc in the space before the shell. * dc 5 in the shell and sc in the space between the shells* now repeat *to* to the end of the sc in the space after the last shell and dc 2 on top of the ch 3

Finishing Off: Sew 3 buttons on the right side of the yoke and use the space at the end of the rows for the buttonholes or sc up the back side and work 3 ch 2 loops for the buttonholes on the left side. Sc across the neckline and down the other side to finish

Chapter 4 – Rainbow Sugar Fairy Dress

Size: 18-24 months

Skill Level: Beginner-Intermediate

Materials: 5 complimentary colors of sport weight yarn and a size 5mm crochet hook

Pattern

Bodice

Ch 56

Ch 3, dc 2, ch 1, then *skip 1 ch and dc 3 then ch 1 and skip 1 ch then dc 3* repeat *to* to the end of the row and finish with sl st on top of the ch 3. There is now 14 dc 3 clusters and 14 gaps.

Change color and ch 4 then dc 3 in the first gap (this is the 1st increase).

Ch 1, dc 3 in the next gap and ch 1 then dc 3 in the next gap and ch 1, dc 3, ch 1 and dc 3 in the next gap (this is the 2nd increase)

Ch1, dc 3 in the next gap and ch 1, dc 3 in the next gap then ch 1 dc 3 in the next gap and ch1, dc 3, ch 1, dc 3 in the next gap (this is the 3rd increase)

Ch 1, dc 3 in the next gap then ch 1, dc 3 in the next gap and ch 1, dc 3, ch 1, dc 3 in the next gap (this is the 4th increase)

Now continue with the dc 3 clusters and ch 1 to the end of the row and finish with dc 2 and a sl st on the top of the ch3

The body of the dress is worked with dc 3 clusters in each ch 1 space between the dc 3 cluster of the previous row, and dc 3, ch 1, dc 3 in each ch space of each increase.

Each row is worked in a different color, so change color for each row. Work approximately 7 rows like this, do more or less to obtain the size needed. Then close the armholes with a sl st

Skirt

The skirt is worked with dc 3 clusters in each gap with no ch1 between until the next increase. Skip the gaps until the next increase (armhole) and dc 3 cluster in each gap to next increase and skip all the gaps to the next increase (armhole) then finish with a sl st on top of the ch3

Now work all the rows with dc 3 in each gap and ch 2 between the dc clusters. Work 17 rows or continue until the desired length is reached

Edging

Work a shell edging with dc 4 in each gap of the collar and a sl st on the middle dc of the dc 3 cluster, now dc 5 in each gap and sl st in the middle dc of the 3 dc cluster of the armholes and the skirt

Chapter 5 – Open Work Princess Dress

Size: Newborn to One Month

Skill: Intermediate

Material: 2 skein of yarn, one for the trim and one for the dress, ribbon for the bodice, 2 small buttons, hook sizes K and N, yarn needle and sewing needle and some thread

Notes: Decrease for this dress is as follows: Draw up a loop in the st then draw up a loop in the next st now work both loops off hook. Pico Stitch for this dress as follows: Sc then ch 3 and sl st in the first ch then sc in the same sp. Shell stitch for this dress as follows: Work 5 dc in the same st or sp

Pattern

Use the smaller hook and white yarn, or whichever color you choose ch 42

Row 1: Dc in the fourth ch from the hook, dc 4, then (dc, ch 2, dc) in the next ch, dc 5, then (dc, ch 2, dc) in the next ch, dc 16, then (dc, ch 2, dc) in the next ch, dc 5 then (dc, ch 2, dc) in the next ch, now dc 5 then ch 3 and turn

Row 2: Dc 5 then (2 dc, ch 2, 2 dc) in the next ch-2 sp then dc 7, now (2 dc, ch 2, 2 dc) in the next ch-2 sp then dc 18 and (2 dc, ch 2, 2 dc) in the next ch-2 sp then dc 7 and (2 dc, ch 2, 2 dc) in the next ch-2 sp then dc 6, ch 3 and turn

Row 3: Dc 7, then (2 dc, ch 2, 2 dc) in the next ch-2 sp then dc 11 and (2 dc, ch 2, 1 dc) in the next ch-2 sp then dc 22 and (1 dc, ch 2, 2 dc) in the next ch-2 sp now dc 11 and (2 dc, ch 2, 2 dc) in the next ch-2 sp then dc 8, ch 3 and turn

Row 4: Dc 9 then (1 dc, ch 2, 1 dc) in the next ch-2 sp now dc 15 then (1 dc, ch 2, 1 dc) in the next ch-2 sp now dc 24 then (1 dc, ch 2, 1 dc) in the next ch-2 sp then dc 15 and (1 dc, ch 2, 1 dc) in the next ch-2 sp and dc 10 the ch 3 and turn

Join Bodice

Dc in each dc to the first ch-2 sp. * Dc in next sp then ch 3 and skip sleeve sts, dc in the next ch-2 sp* repeat *to* once. Dc in each dc to the next ch-2 sp then dc in each remaining dc and end with a sl st in the top of the beg ch-3. From this point forward, do not turn work.

Skirt

Rnd 1: Ch 3 and skip the 1 st now shell then skip the 1 st * dc and skip the 1 st then shell and skip the 1 st* repeat from *to* around and end with a sl st in the top of the beg ch-3

Rnd 2: Ch 3 and shell in the center dc of the shell * dc then shell in the center dc of the next shell* repeat from *to*around and end with a sl st as before

Now switch to the larger hook

Rnds 3 – 7: Repeat Rnd 2

Rnds 8 – 9: Ch 4 then shell in the center dc of the next shell and ch 1 now *dc then ch 1 and shell then ch 1* repeat from *to* around and end as before. Fasten off the yarn.

Picot Edging

Ch 1 then sc in the same sp and sc in each dc and the ch-1 sp around. Now work the Picot in the center dc of each shell

Sleeve Edging

Attach pink yarn at back of right sleeve and ch-2 sp then sc in same sp now *skip the 1 st and shell then skip the 1 st and sc*, then repeat from *to* 3 times (4 shells). Now work 3 sc across underarm then fasten off the yarn. Repeat for the left sleeve and start at ch-2 sp on the front of the sleeve

Neck and Back Opening Edging

Attach the pink yarn to the neck at the top of the left back

Row 1: Sc in the same sp and work sc across the neck then make a dec in each base ch of the first row's increases (4 dec) now sc evenly down the right back and work two ch-3 buttonholes. Sc up the left back and end with a sl st in the first sc and do not turn

Row 2: Ch 1 and sc in the same sp now *skip the 1 st and shell then skip the 1 st and sc* repeat from *to* across and end with a sl st in the sc at the top of the right back. (8 shells) Now fasten off the yarn

Bodice Shell Ruffle

With the right side facing you, fold the bodice at the second and third rows and attach yarn at the left back between the two rows. Work between the sts of the folded rows, ch 1 then sc in the same sp *shell in the next st and sc in the next st* now repeat from *to* around the bodice (22 shells) and fasten off the yarn

Weave in all of the yarn ends then sew two small buttons at the left back opening. Now weave ribbon through the dcs of the Bodice Joining row and tie in a bow

Chapter 6 – Bonus Appliques and Headband

These appliques are simple to make and they really boost the princess power of the dresses in this book. With a little practice, you will be creating your own appliques, but for now, these should keep you busy. Appliques are great because they have so many uses! Here is a list of things you can do with your appliques:

- Add them to a dress
- Add them to a headband/hat/ or other accessory
- Add them to a baby blanket
- Make a mobile for the baby's crib!
- Use them for all four and you will have a theme going!
- Use the star applique to make a crochet princess wand/scepter (she is going to need one of these when she wears her princess dresses and princess headband crown)

Easy Breezy Daisy

Skill Level: Beginner

Materials: Yellow and white yarn or any two colors you choose, sport weight yarn works best, and US size H hook

Pattern

Use yellow first, ch 3, join to make a circle

Rnd 1: Ch 1 (this counts as a sc) now make 7 sc in the middle of the yellow ring and join with a sl st to the first sc

Rnd 2: Ch 1 then sc in same st, now 2 sc in each of the remaining sc for a total of 16 sc. Cut the thread and weave in ends

Rnd 3: Join the white yarn in any sc. Work in the back loops only and ch 3 then tr in the same sc now sc and tr then ch 3 and sl st (this is the first petal) *sl st in the next sc then ch 3 and tr in the same sc now sl st to the next sc then tr then ch 3 and sl st in the same sc* (second petal made). Now repeat from *to* until a total of 8 petals are made then cut thread and weave in ends.

Royal Roses

Skill Level: Beginner

Materials: Sport weight or baby weight yarn any color, US size H hook and a yarn needle

Pattern

Leave a 10" length of yarn for sewing and chain 36

Row 1: Dc, ch 2 and dc in the sixth ch from the hook (the 5 skipped chs count as the first dc plus ch 2), * ch 2 and skip the next 2 chs then dc, ch 2 and dc in the next ch* now repeat from *to* across for 22 sps.

Row 2: Ch 3 then turn now 5 dc in the next ch then skip 2 sp and sc in the next ch then skip 2 sp now *6 dc in the next ch skip 2 sp and sc in the next ch then skip 2 sp* repeat *to* 5 times then *9 dc in the next ch skip 2 sp then sc in the next sp* repeat *to* 5 times then tie off and leave a 10" length for sewing.

Thread the yarn needle with the 10" yarn from the beginning. With the right side facing you, begin with first petal made, roll the rose; you will see the rose beginning to form as you roll, then sew to secure. Then thread the yarn needle with ending 10" piece of yarn and sew to secure.

Twinkle-Twinkle Stars

Skill Level: Beginner-Intermediate

Materials: Sport weight yarn any color, US size H hook

Special Stitches

Picot: ch 3 and insert the hook in the 3rd ch from the hook now yarn over and draw the yarn through the stitch and through the loop on the hook

Pattern

5 ch and join with a sl st to form ring

Round 1: 3 ch (this will count as the first dc st) then dc 14 into the center of the ring then join with a sl st to the beginning ch 3 (now there are 15 dc stitches in ring)

Round 2: *7 ch then sc in the 4th ch from the hook then hdc in the next ch then dc in the next ch then tr in the next ch now skip 2 dc sts and sl st in the 3rd dc st* repeat *to* 4 more times then sl st in the first ch st at the beginning of the round (now you have 5 points of the star)

Round 3: *sc in each ch st along one side of a point of the star now sc 2 then ch 3 picot and sc all in the ch 3 space at the top of the star point. sc in each st along the other side of star point and sc at the base of the point* now repeat *to* 4 more times and sl st in the first sc at the beginning of the round. Cut the yarn and fasten off then weave in the ends.

Tie on Baby Headband

Size: Adjustable with ties

Skill Level: Beginner

Materials: Small amount of sport weight yarn, 5mm crochet hook

Pattern

ch 70

Row 1: sc in the 2nd ch from the hook then sc in the next 14 sts now ch 3 and skip the next st then dc in the following st. *ch 1 then skip the next st and dc in the next st* repeat *to* 18 more times then sc in the next st and sc in the remaining 14 sts. Now turn the work

Row 2: ch 1 then sl st in the next st and sl st in next 13 sts now ch 3 and dc in the first ch 1 space then ch 1 *dc then ch 1 in the next ch 1 space* repeat *to* for remaining ch 1 spaces and sl st in the last 15 sts as in row 1 then fasten off the yarn and weave in your ends

The picture shows a flower decoration, you can make any of the appliques in this section and attach it to the headband. The size is adjustable by tying the long ends.

Conclusion

Frilly dresses for a baby girl are a must have and now you have the skills you need to create your own. The combinations for creating a beautiful one of a kind dress is endless with the patterns you have learned. You can use the bonus appliques for personalizing each one. You can even create a set using the headband pattern; just choose complimentary colors and match the headband to the dress.

These dresses and personalization options are great for creating a one of a kind gift for a baby shower. You can even create an entire wardrobe for your little princess without breaking the bank. These patterns can be sized up for toddlers with a little increasing to the width and adding rows to the length. Even the headband can be sized up for toddlers with a few extra beginning chains.

Last but not least, these dresses can be altered to create crochet tops; just shorten the length and add some appliques! For a cute long sleeve look, add rounds of crochet beginning at the arm holes and adjust for look and size. If you are really good at making alterations, you can even use these to make the beginning of a cute cardigan.

These patterns will serve as the basis for many adorable items for baby. By matching colors and appliques you will have an endless supply of style for her and enough crochet projects to keep you busy and happy.

Crochet Mandala Patterns

Introduction

You are about to learn how to make the most functional item in your crochet repertoire. Even if you don't have a repertoire yet, these mandala rugs will be the beginning of your crochet legacy! Each pattern is versatile and beginner friendly.

As you learn the stitches and create the patterns, you will begin to realize that with a bit of tweaking, you can make them bigger or smaller. That's the beauty of these mandalas. You can make a rug, matching pillows, and adorable table colors with one pattern and a color scheme.

Every pattern is easy to read and a breeze to create. The stitch guide, yarn and hook guides, will help you as you learn. You can look back on these guides whenever you need to. The yarn and hook guide will also be helpful if you decided to create some doilies or table colors and don't want to use the yarn size you used for the rugs.

The color schemes used for each rug can be re-arranged to compliment any décor. Just insert the color you prefer into the pattern when it calls for a color change. Creating your own rugs and accessories couldn't be easier than this!

You will learn to use different size crochet hooks, and varying size yarns. From T-shirt yarn to bulky yarn, each mandala has its own unique texture and pattern. Heavy, bulkier yarns will add loft and size to the rug, but if you use a thinner yarn, the mandala will be more delicate and lacey.

Before washing the finished project, check for color fastness by using a small amount of detergent in an inconspicuous area. Follow the washing directions on the yarn packaging. Use one brand of yarn when making the rug, do not switch brands when switching colors; cleaning instructions for different brands may differ and your rug may end up un-washable.

After you finish each mandala it may be a bit out of shape. You can learn to block the project to shape it. If the yarn package says it is ok to iron it, you can use an iron to shape the rug and remove any bumps. You can even throw it in the washing machine and dry it on a blocking rack to shape it.

The crochet stitch guide covers just about every stitch you will need to use. If there are stitches in the pattern that are not covered by the crochet stitch guide, a special note for the stitch used will be found in the pattern itself. The stitch guide and the hook guide have information in both US and British terms.

Chapter 1 – Crochet Stitch Guide

CROCHET ABBREVIATIONS & TERMS

beg = beginning	hdc = half double crochet	sp(s) = space(s)
bg = block	htr = half treble crochet	st(s) = stitch(es)
cc = contrast colour	inc = increase	tog = together
ch = chain	rep = repeat	tr = treble crochet
dc = double crochet	rnd = round	tr tr = treble treble crochet
dec = decrease	sc = single crochet	ws = wrong side
dtr = double treble crochet	sl st = slip stitch	yo = yarn over

[ ] = work instructions within brackets as many times as directed

( ) = work instructions within parentheses as many times as directed

* = repeat the instructions following the single asterisk as directed

* * = repeat the instructions between the asterisks as many times as directed

Chapter 2 – Crochet Hook and Yarn Guide

USA	English	Metric
14	6	0.60
12	5	0.75
10	4	1.00
—	3	1.25
6	2.5	1.50
4	2	1.75
B	14	2.00
C	12	2.50
D	11	3.00
E	9	3.50
F	8	4.00
G	7	4.50
H	6	5.00
I	5	5.50
J	4	6.00
K	2	7.00
—	1/0	8.00
—	2/0	9.00
P	3/0	10.00

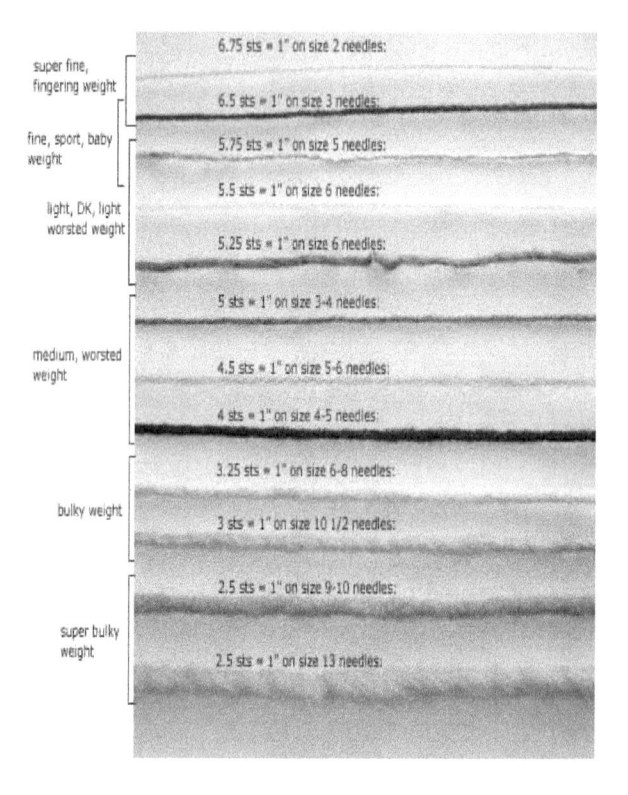

Weight Category	Gauge
super fine, fingering weight	6.75 sts = 1" on size 2 needles
	6.5 sts = 1" on size 3 needles
fine, sport, baby weight	5.75 sts = 1" on size 5 needles
	5.5 sts = 1" on size 6 needles
light, DK, light worsted weight	5.25 sts = 1" on size 6 needles
medium, worsted weight	5 sts = 1" on size 3-4 needles
	4.5 sts = 1" on size 5-6 needles
	4 sts = 1" on size 4-5 needles
bulky weight	3.25 sts = 1" on size 6-8 needles
	3 sts = 1" on size 10 1/2 needles
super bulky weight	2.5 sts = 1" on size 9-10 needles
	2.5 sts = 1" on size 13 needles

Chapter 3 – Shades of Pastel Mandala Rug

Skill Level – Beginner, Intermediate

Materials – You will need a 3mm crochet hook and four pastels, or light colored sport weight yarns; one skein for each color and a pair of scissors.

Note for Special Stitches –

hdc v-stitch (hdcv) – half double crochet v stitch (hdc, chain 1, hdc)

3dc cluster- 3 double crochet cluster

3tr cluster- 3 treble crochet cluster

Puff stitch

In each round you start with a 3 dc cluster or a 3 treble cluster. Chain 2 for the 3dc (counts as the first dc) and chain 3 for the 3tr (counts as first treble). You will change colors after each round.

Pattern –

Round 1 - Ch 6 and make a ring using a slst

Round 2   Ch 1 then sc 13 into the ring and then fasten with a slst in the first sc.

Round 3 – In the first sc make a 3tr cluster then ch 1 in the next sc, now * 3dc and ch 1* repeat * to * until the round is complete. Now tie off with a slst in the top of the first 3tr cluster and attach a new color in the first 3tr with a slst

Round 4 - ch 1 and then 3 sc *skip the cluster 3 sc in the next ch space* repeat * to * until the round is complete then tie off with a slst in the first sc. Now attach the new color in the first 3tr with a slst

Round 5 - sc in every sc and then tie off with a slst in the first sc and change color

Round 6 - ch 2 then*ch 1 and hdc in the next sc* repeat * to * until the round is complete, then tie off with a slst in the 2nd chain of the first hdc and change color

Round 7 - ch 2, then *ch 2 and hdc in the next ch space and then ch 2* repeat *to* until the row is complete then tie off with a slst in the 2nd ch of the first hdc and change color

Round 8 - sc 2 in every ch space and then tie off the yarn with a slst and change color

Round 9 - sc in every sc then tie off with a slst and change yarn

Round 10 - ch2 hdc in every stitch, tie off with a slst and change yarn

Round 11 - ch2 then *ch 2 and skip 1 hdc then hdc in the next stitch* repeat *to* until the round is complete then tie off with a slst and attach another color

Round 12 - ch 1 then sc 3 in every chain space and tie off with a slst and attach another color

Round 13 - make a 3dc cluster then *ch 1 and skip one sc then 3dc cluster in the next sc and then ch 1 * repeat *to* until the round is complete. On the last round, leave out the last two chains and tie off with a slst in the first 3dc cluster and change color

Round 14 - make a 3dc cluster then chain 2 and *3dc cluster then chain 2* repeat *to* until the round is complete then tie off with a slst in top of your first cluster. Now change color

Round 15 – ch 3 then hdc in the same chain space (your first hdc v-stitch). Skip the cluster then *hdc and ch 1 then hdc* in next chain space, repeat *to* until the round is complete, then tie off with a slst in the 2nd chain of the ch3. Change color

Round 16 - ch 3 and hdc in same ch space, then hdc v-stitch in every hdcv and tie off with a slst in the 2nd ch in the starting ch3. Change color

Round 17 - 3dc cluster then chain 2 and 3dc cluster in next hdcv, then tie off with a slst in the top of the 3dc cluster. Change color

Round 18 - ch 2 then 2 hdc in the same ch space and *in the next ch space, hdc 3*, now tie off with a slst and change color

Round 19 - ch 1 then sc in every hdc, tie off with a slst and change color

Round 20 - ch 3 then hdc in the same sc, *Skip one sc and hdcv in the next sc* repeat *to* until the round is complete, at the last hdcv, skip the two las sc and tie off with a slst then change color

Round 21 - Repeat round 16 and change color

Round 22 - puff stitch then chain 2 and *puff stitch then ch 2* now repeat *to* until the round is complete, tie off with a slst in the top of the first puff stitch and change color out.

Round 23 – repeat round 14 then tie off with a slst and change color

Round 24 - sc in every hdc then tie off with a slst and change color

Edging

Round 25 - *ch 2 then skip one sc and ss in the next sc* repeat *to* until the round is complete

Chapter 4 – Pink T-Shirt Mandala Rug

Skill Level – Beginner, Intermediate

Materials – Three skeins of T-shirt yarn in two colors, 15mm crochet hook, a large needle for sewing ends and a pair of scissors

Pattern -

Round 1 - make a magic ring with the main yarn color then slst to secure and ch3, then 11dc in the ring. Pull closed and secure with a slst in the 3rd ch from the 1st ch3

Round 2 - ch 3 then dc in the same stitch, now work 2dc in each stitch around and join with a slst on the top of the starting ch3

Round 3 - ch 3, then 2dc in the next stitch and *1dc then 2dc* repeat *to* until the round is complete then join with a slst

Round 4 – ch 3 then ch 2 and skip a stitch then *1dc and ch2 then skip 1 stitch* repeat *to* until the round is complete then join with a slst

Round 5 - ch 3 then 2 dc in the ch2 space and 1dc in the underlying dc now *inc, 1dc in dc* repeat *to* until the round is complete then join with a slst

Round 6 - change color then ch 3 now 1 dc in the next stitch and 2dc in the next stitch and *2dc, inc* repeat *to* until the round is complete then join with a slst

Round 7 - ch 3 the chain 2 and skip a stitch now *1dc and ch2 then sk 1 st* repeat *to* until the round is complete then join with a slst

Round 8 - ch 3 then 2 dc in the ch2 space and dc in the underlying dc, then *inc, 1dc in the dc* repeat *to* until the round is complete then tie off with a slst and change color

Round 9 – ch 3 then dc in the next stitch and *1dc* repeat until the round is complete and join with a slst. Join with a slip stitch

Round 10 - ch 3 then 1dc in ch2 space now 1dc in the underlying dc and 2dc in the ch2 space and *1dc in dc and 1dc in ch2 space then 1dc in dc and inc* repeat until the round is complete then tie off with a slst and change color

Round 11 – ch 3 then 1dc in the next stitch, and *1dc* repeat from *to* until the round is complete then join with a slst

Round 12 - ch 3 then ch 2 and skip a stitch, then *1dc and ch2 then sk 1 st* repeat until the round is complete then join with a slst

Round 13 - ch 3 then 1dc in the ch2 space and 1dc in the underlying dc and 2dc in the ch2 space, now *1dc in dc and 1dc in the ch2 space, then 1dc in dc, and inc* repeat *to* until the round is complete then tie off with a slst and change color

Round 14 - ch 3 then 1dc in the next stitch, and *1dc* repeat *to* until the round is complete then join with a slst

Round 15 -ch 3 then ch 2 and skip a stitch, then *1dc and ch2 then sk 1 st* repeat *to* until the round is complete then join with a slst

Round 16 - ch 3 then 1dc in the ch2 space and 1dc in the underlying dc and 1dc in the ch2 space then 1dc in the underlying dc and 2dc in the ch2 space, then *1dc in dc and 1dc in ch2 space and 1dc in dc now 1dc in the ch2 space and 1dc in dc then inc* until the round is complete then join with a slst

Round 17 - ch 1 and sc in the same stitch now skip two stitches and 6dc in the next stitch then skip two stitches, and *1sc then sk 2 st and 6dc then sk 2 st* repeat until the round is complete then join with a slst and fasten off

Finishing off the rug -

Flip the rug over and with the yarn needle, weave in all the ends under the dc's then cut the yarn ends

Chapter 5 – Star Shower Mandala Rug

Skill Level – Beginner, Intermediate

Materials – Worsted or sport weight yarn, 3.50 mm hood and scissors

Pattern -

Foundation Row – ch 6 and slst to the first chain to form a circle

Round 1 - ch 2 then 2dc cluster and ch 3 now *3dc cluster and ch 3* repeat *to* 5 times then close with a slst and cut the yarn with the scissor

Round 2 - 3ch then 3dc and 1ch into a ch3 space then *into next 3ch space, 4dc then 1ch* repeat *to* 5 times now slst to finish

Round 3 - join yarn in the 1st and 2nd dc on any 4dc group then 3ch and 1dc into the same space then 2dc into each of the next 2 spaces 8ch and then *2dc into each space between the dc on the next 4dc group and then 8ch* repeat *to* 5 times and slst to close

Round 4 - Join the yarn with a slst into the first dc space then slst from the front to the back loops on the next 5dc then *into the 8ch space, and 1sc then 1hdc and 3dc then 1tr and 3ch then 1tr and 3dc then 1hdc and 1sc (Petal formed) now 1 slst from the front and back loops on next 6dc* repeat *to* 5 times then slst into the last 8ch space and 1sc the 1hdc and 3dc now 1tr then 3ch and 1tr then 3dc and 1hdc now 1sc and cut the yarn

To end this round, use a yarn needle and pull the yarn through from the front to the back on the first slst then pull to tighten. Now thread the yarn through the back loops on the next 5 slst's

Round 5 - Join the yarn into the 3rd dc on Row 3 and 3ch then 1dc into the next dc and *3ch then 1sc into the first dc on the Petal then 1hdc into the next dc and 1dc into each of the next 2 stitches, now 2dc and 1tr then 3ch and 1tr now 2dc into 3ch space and 1dc into each of the next 2 stitches, now 1hdc into the next dc and 1sc into the next dc then 3ch, now 1dc into each of the 3rd and 4th dc on row 3* repeat *to* 5 times then 3ch and 1sc into the first dc on the Petal and 1hdc into the next dc and 1dc into each of the next 2 stitches, now 2dc and 1tr then 3ch and 1tr now 2dc into the 3ch space and 1dc into each of the next 2 stitches now 1hdc into the next dc and 1sc into the next dc and 3ch into the top of the 3ch at the start of the row to close

Round 6 - Join yarn in the center of any middle 2dc and 3ch then 1dc now *3ch and 1sc into the first dc on the Petal and 1hdc into the next dc and 1dc into each of the next 3 stitches then 2dc and 3ch then 2dc into the 3ch space then 1dc into each of the next 3 stitches and 1hdc into the next dc then 1sc into the next dc and 3ch now 2dc into the center of the middle 2dc grouping* now repeat *to* 5 times and 3ch then 1sc into the first dc on the Petal then 1hdc into the next dc and 1dc into each of the next 3 stitches then 2dc and 3ch then 2dc into the 3ch space now 1dc into each of the next 3 stitches then 1hdc into the next dc and 1sc into the next dc and 3ch, now slst into the top of the start 3ch

Round 7 - Join the yarn into the center of any middle 2dc grouping and 1ch then 1sc, now *6ch and 1sc into the first dc on the Petal and 1hdc into the next dc and 1dc into each of the next 3 dc now 2dc and 3ch then 2dc into the 3ch space, then 1dc into each of the next 3 dc and 1hdc into the next dc then 1sc into the next dc and 6ch, then 1 sc into the center of the middle 2dc grouping* now repeat *to* 5 times and 6ch then 1sc into the first dc on the Petal and 1hdc into the next dc and 1dc into each of the next 3 dc, now 2dc and 3ch then 2dc into the 3ch space, now 1dc into each of the next 3 dc and 1hdc into the next dc and 1sc into the next dc then 6ch and slst into the starting 1ch

Round 8 - Join yarn into the first dc on the right hand side of any Petal and 1ch then 1sc into the same dc and 1hdc into the next dc and 1 dc into each of the next

3dc now 2dc and 3ch then 2dc into the 3ch space, now 1dc into each of the next 3dc and 1hdc into the next dc then 1sc into the next dc, now *6ch and 1sc into the 6ch on round 7 then 6ch and 1sc into the 6ch on round 7 then 6ch and 1sc into the first dc on the Petal and 1hdc into the next dc and 1dc into each of the next 3dc now 2dc and 3ch then 2dc into the 3ch space then 1dc into each of the next 3dc, and 1hdc into the next dc then 1sc into the next dc* then repeat *to* 5 times and 6ch then 1sc into the 6ch on round 7 and 6ch then 1sc into the 6ch on round 7 then 6ch and slst into the 1ch at the start of the row

Round 9 - Join the yarn into the 4th dc on the right hand side of any Petal and 3ch then 1dc into the next dc and 2dc then 3ch and 2dc into the 3ch space now 1dc into each of the next 2dc and *6ch and 1sc into the 6ch space* and repeat 3 times, then *6ch and 1dc into the 4th dc on the Petal and 1dc into the next dc now 2dc and 3ch then 2dc into the 3ch space, now 1dc into each of the next 2dc* and repeat *to* 5 times and *6ch then 1sc into the 6ch space* repeat *to* 3 times now 6ch

Round 10 - Join yarn into the third dc on the right side of any petal and 2ch then 1hdc into the next dc and 2hdc then 2ch and 2hdc into the 3ch space then 1hdc into each of the next 2dc and *6ch and 1sc into the 6ch space and 6ch then 4dc into the next 6ch space and 4dc into the next 6ch space then 6ch and 1sc into the 6ch space and 6ch then 1hdc into the third dc on the Petal and 1hdc into the next dc now 2hdc and 2ch then 2hdc into the 3ch space and 1hdc into each of the next 2dc* repeat *to*5 times, now 6ch and 1sc into the 6ch space and 6ch then 4dc into the next 6ch space and 4dc into the next 6ch space then 6ch and 1sc into the 6ch space and 6ch then slst into the top of the 2ch at the start of the row

Round 11 - Join the yarn into the third hdc on the right side of any Petal and 2ch then 1hdc into the next hdc and 3hdc into the 2ch space then 1hdc into each of the next 2hdc, now *6ch and 3dc into the 6ch space then 6ch then (1tr into each of the next 4 dc) 2 times and 6ch then skip the first 6ch space and 3dc into the next 6ch space then 6ch and 1hdc into the third hdc then 1hdc into the next hdc and 3hdc into the 2ch space and 1hdc into each of the next 2hdc* now repeat *to* 5 times and slst into the top of the 2ch at the start of the row

Round Join the yarn between the 3rd and 4th hdc on the right hand side of any Petal and 2ch then 1hdc between the 4th and the 5th hdc now *1ch and 6dc, into each of the next two 6ch spaces and 1ch then skip 1st tr on round 11 and 1tr into each of the next 6 tr and 1ch then 6dc into each of the next two 6ch spaces and 1ch then 1hdc between the 3rd and the 4th hdc now 1hdc between the 4th and the 5th hdc* then repeat *to* 5 times and 1ch then 6dc and 1ch into each of the next 2 6ch spaces and skip 1st tr on round 11 and 1tr into each of the next 6 tr and 1ch and 6dc then 1ch into each of the next 2 6ch spaces now slst into the top of the 2ch at the start of the row to close

Round 13 - Join the yarn between the 2hdc at the top of the Petal and 2ch then *1hdc into the 1ch space and 1hdc into each of the next 6dc and 1dc into each of the next 6dc and 1tr into each of the next 6tr now 1dc into each of the next 6dc and 1hdc into each of the next 6dc and 1hdc into the 1 ch space and 1hdc into the space between the 2hdc at top of Petal* now repeat *to* 5 times and 1hdc into the 1ch space and 1hdc into each of the next 6dc and 1dc into each of the next 6dc then 1tr into each of the next 6tr and 1dc into each of the next 6dc and 1hdc into each of the next 6dc and 1hdc into the 1 ch space now slst into the top of the 2ch at the start of the row to close

Round 14 - Join the yarn into the second tr of any 6tr sequence on round 13 then 4ch and 1tr into each of the next 4tr and 1dc into each of the next 13 stitches and 1tr into each of the next 2hdc and 1dc into each of the next 13 stitches and *1tr into each of the next 5tr then 1dc into each of the next 13 stitches and 1tr into each of the next 2hdc and 1dc into each of the next 13 stitches* now repeat *to* 5 times then slst into the top of the 4ch at the start of the row to close

Round 15 - Join the yarn in the space between any 2tr at the top of the Petal and 5ch then skip two spaces and 1 sc in the next space now *4ch and skip 2 spaces, then 1sc in the next space* repeat *to* until the last 2 spaces then 4ch and slst into the 1st chain at the start of the row

Round 16 - Join the yarn in any 4ch space and 3ch then 2dc in the same space and 1ch now *3dc and 1ch in the next 4ch space* and repeat *to* to the end of the row and slst into the top of the 3ch at the start of the row to close

Round 17 - Join the yarn in the 2nd dc of any 3dc group on round 16 and 1ch then 1sc in the same space as the join then 1ch now *dc a spike on the left of the sc in round 15 and dc a spike to the right of the sc in round 15 now 1ch and 1sc into the second dc of the next 3dc group and 1ch* repeat *to* until the end of the row then slst into the 1ch at the start of the row to close

Round 18 - Join the yarn with a slst in the 1ch space to the left of any crossover spike and slst in the next 1ch space and *6ch then slst into the 4th ch from the hook and slst into the 1ch space to the left of the next crossover stitch and slst into the next 1ch* repeat *to* to the right of the last crossover spike and 6ch then slst into the 4th ch from the hook and slst into the slst at the start of the row

Chapter 6 – Chunky Mandala Rug

Skill Level – Beginner to Intermediate

Materials - A US size Q or 15mm hook, 500 yards of super bulky yarn in two colors, 250 yards each, any color you choose, a yarn needle, scissors

Note - Starting in Round 2 with Color B, crochet over the unused color by holding it behind the row at the bottom and crocheting over it and carrying it along until it is used again.

Pattern -

Round 1 – Begin with color A and ch 6 then join with a slst to form a ring now ch 2 and dc 12 in the ring then join to the first dc with a slst

Round 2 - ch 2 and dc2tog over the first two stiches and finish the stitch with Color B now 3 dc between the post of the previous stitch and the next stitch and finish the last stitch with Color A then *Dc2tog and finish the stitch with Color B then 3 dc between post of the previous and the next stitch and finish the last stitch with Color A and repeat from * to the end and join with a slst to the top of the first dc2tog

Round 3 - ch 1 and sc in the first stitch and finish the stitch with Color B then skip the next stitch and 5 dc in the next stitch and finish the last stitch with Color A and skip the next stitch then *sc in the next stitch and finish the stitch with Color B now skip the next stitch and 5 dc in the next stitch and finish the last stitch with Color A and skip the next stitch then repeat from * to the end and join with a slst to the top of the first stitch

Round 4 - ch 2 and (2 dc and finish last stitch with Color B then 2 dc and finish the last stitch with Color A and 2 dc and finish the last stitch with Color B) in the first stitch now skip the next 2 stitches and sc in the next stitch and finish with Color A then *skip the next 2 stitches and (2 dc and finish with last stitch with Color B then 2 dc and finish the last stitch with Color A then 2 dc and finish the last stitch with Color B) in the next stitch then skip the next 2 stitches and sc in the next stitch and finish with Color A now repeat from * to the end and join with a slst to the top of the first stitch

Round 5 – ch 2 and 2 dc in the first stitch then 2 dc in the next stitch and finish the last stitch with Color B then dc2tog and finish the stitch with Color A then 2 dc in the next stitch and 2 dc in the next stitch and finish the last stitch with Color B and dc in the next stitch and finish with Color A now * 2 dc in the next stitch then 2 dc in the next stitch and finish the last stitch with Color B now dc2tog and finish the stitch with Color A then 2 dc in the next stitch and 2 dc in the next stitch and finish the last stitch with Color B now dc in next the stitch and finish with Color A then repeat from * to the end and join with a slst to the top of the first stitch

Round 6 - ch 2 and *2 dc between the post of the next and the following stitch then ch 1 and skip the next 2 stitches and 2 dc between the post of the previous and the next stitch then finish the last stitch with Color B and skip the next stitch and sc in the next stitch and finish with Color A now repeat from * to the end and join with a slst to the top of the first stitch

Round 7 ch 2 and dc2tog in the first two stitches and finish with Color B then 3 dc in the ch space and finish the last stitch with Color A then dc2tog and finish with Color B and 3 dc in the next stitch and finish with Color A then *dc2tog and finish with Color B now 3 dc in the ch space and finish the last stitch with Color A then dc2tog and finish with Color B now 3 dc in the next stitch and finish with Color A then repeat from * to the end and join with a slst to the top of the first stitch

Round 8 - ch 2 and dc in the first stitch and finish with Color B and dc in the next 3 stitches then finish the last stitch with Color A now *dc in the next stitch and finish with Color B and dc in the next 3 stitches then finish the last stitch with Color A and repeat from * to the end and join with a slst to the top of the first stitch

Round 9 - ch 1 and sc in the first stitch then finish with Color B then skip the next stitch and (2 dc then ch 1 and 2 dc) in the next stitch and finish with the last stitch with Color A now skip the next stitch and *sc in the first stitch and finish with the Color B and skip the next stitch and (2 dc then ch 1 and 2 dc) in the next stitch and finish the last stitch with Color A and skip the next stitch then repeat from * to the end and join with a slst to the top of the first stitch

Round 10 - ch 1 and sc in the first stitch and finish with Color B then skip the next 2 stitches and 5 dc in the ch space then finish the last stitch with Color A and skip the next 2 stitches now *sc in the next stitch and finish with Color B then skip the next 2 stitches and 5 dc in the ch space then finish the last stitch with Color A and skip the next 2 stitches now repeat from * to the end and join with a slst to the top of the first stitch

Round 11 - ch 2 and 3 dc in the first stitch and finish the last stitch with Color B and *skip the next 2 stitches then sc in the next stitch and finish with Color A then skip the next 2 stitches and 5 dc in the next stitch then finish with Color B and repeat from * ending with 2 dc with Color A worked in the same stitch as the first 3 stitches of the round and join with a slst to the top of the first stitch

Round 12 - ch 2, and dc in the first stitch then dc in the next 2 stitches and finish the last stitch with Color B now * 2 dc in the next stitch and finish the last stitch with Color A and dc in the next 5 stitches and finish the last stitch with Color B and repeat from * until 2 stitches remain then dc in the last 2 stitches with Color A and join with a slst to the top of the first stitch

Round 13 - ch 2 then 2 dc in the first stitch and finish the last stitch with Color B then skip the next 2 stitches and *2 dc in the next stitch then 2 dc in the next stitch and finish the last stitch with Color A now skip the next 2 stitches and 3 dc in the next stitch and finish the last stitch with Color B and skip the next 2 stitches then repeat from * ending with a dc in the same stitch as the first stitch of the round and join with a slst to the top of the first stitch using Color B

Round 14 - leave Color A behind now and don't enclose it, use Color B to slst in the Front Loop of each stitch around then cut Color B and join to the first slst of the round

Round 15 - pick up Color A and slst in the FL of each stitch of round 13 and behind the stitches of round 14 then cut Color A and join to the first slst of the round

Conclusion

The rug patterns you now know can be used to create thousands of rugs, doilies, and even table covers! Adjusting the yarn size and hook size will give you endless combinations. For larger rugs, continue enlarging until you are happy with the size, for smaller sizes, stop when you have reached the size you want.

Each mandala that you have learned can also be done in a much smaller size. Making a bunch of small mandalas then sewing them together is a great way to create a beautiful, colorful, afghan or lap throw. You can even use these mandalas to create pillows or cushions by putting two mandalas back to back and sewing them before stuffing.

These patterns are perfect for making gifts for any occasion. Use neutral colors and the finished rug will match any décor. Friends and family will love the interesting patterns and the love you put into each creation. Your new crochet skills will help you create endless décor and functional items. The wide variety of things you can create with these mandala patterns will keep you busy year round.

Afghans Crochet in One Day

Introduction

With this book you will learn how to crochet beautiful afghans that can be completed in one day. They may take only one day to complete but they look like you have been crocheting for weeks! Each pattern can be made any length you want, if you want a bigger afghan just add rows until you are happy with the size.

The pictures are for stitch reference; the colors are up to you. You can use the colors shown in the picture or choose a palate to match your décor, the choice is yours. Included in this book is a flower with leaves applique that you can use to personalize any afghan you want.

Some of the patterns are perfect for keeping you cozy while reading or watching TV, these are called Lapghans. A Lapghan is perfect for throwing over your lap at outdoor sporting events or throwing over your shoulders while you crochet another awesome afghan!

Afghans are great for gift giving. You can personalize the color to compliment the recipient's personality or décor. If you are making one for a baby, you can even personalize it by embroidering the birth date somewhere on the afghan. An afghan with a date is a wonderful shower gift for baby or for a soon to be bride.

The yarn weight used for each pattern is listed under materials. Yarn weight can determine how quickly a project can be worked; the thicker the yarn and the larger the hook, the faster it works up. Read the labels on the yarn for washing and care instructions; acrylic yarns are easy to care for and can be washed and dried on low. Some yarns such as wool cannot be washed or dried in a dryer; the instructions are on the label.

If the project uses more than one ball or skein of yarn it is important that you purchase it all at once. Many yarns are labeled with a dye lot; the dye lot ensures that the skein or ball is a perfect color match created in one dye lot. This information is on the label; it is important if you want your afghan to be uniform in color.

If this is going to be your first crochet project, take your time and read through the crochet terms and hook guide. Patterns are written with abbreviations for the type of stitches used. Practice some of the stitches in the guide so you are familiar with them before you begin your project. If you are unfamiliar with the stitches, a quick internet search will provide how-to videos.

Gauge is another important part of crocheting an afghan. The gauge is all about stitch size and the size of the finished project. Use the hook size listed for each pattern and practice making the stitches uniform, not too tight, and not too lose. As long as the stitches are uniform in size and shape your afghan will look great and you can always add more rows or remove rows to customize the finished size.

Now it's time to start crocheting and make a few of these comfy, cozy, afghans!

Chapter 1 – Guide for Crochet Terms and Hooks

Before you begin, look over this chapter to familiarize yourself with the abbreviations used in this book. The abbreviations are standard crochet terms, if you do not know the stitches covered in the abbreviations, it is easy to find an online tutorial for beginners.

If you are already familiar with the stitches listed in the abbreviation chart, you will have no problem crocheting the patterns in this book. The patterns for each project use these abbreviations and hook sizes. If you are unfamiliar with these abbreviations, there are many good crochet stitch tutorials online to help you.

Crochet Abbreviations

beg – Beginning	bg - Block
cc – Contrast Color	ch – chain
dc – Double Crochet	dec – Decrease
dtr – Double Treble Crochet	hdc – Half Double Crochet
htr – Half Treble Crochet	inc – Increase
rep – Repeat	rnd – Round
sc – Single Crochet	sl st – Slip Stitch

sp(s) – Space(s)	st(s) – Stitch(s)
tog – Together	tr – Treble Crochet
tr – Treble Crochet	WS – Wrong Side
yo – Yarn Over	RS – Right Side
( ) – Work instructions within the parentheses as many times as directed	* - Repeat instructions following the single asterisk as directed
** - Repeat the instructions within the asterisk as many times as directed	[ ] – Work instructions within the brackets as many times as instructed

Crochet Hook Sizes

U.S.	English	Metric
14	6	0.60
12	5	0.75
10	4	1.00
-	3	1.25
6	2.5	1.50
4	2	1.75

B	14	2.00
C	12	2.50
D	11	3.00
E	9	3.50
F	8	4.00
G	7	4.50
H	6	5.00
I	5	5.50
J	4	6.00
K	2	7.00
-	1/0	8.00
-	2/0	9.00
P	3/0	10.00

Chapter 2 – Chunky Cozy Afghan

Skill Level: Beginner/Easy

Materials: 225 yards or Baby weight or Sport weight yarn, any color. Crochet hook US size P. Scissors.

Notes: Blanket will be around 44"x55" when finished.

Pattern:

Ch 60

Row 1: Do not turn and count back 4 stitches from the hook now make 2 dc in the same chain then skip a chain then 2 dc in the next chain and skip a chain, continue this pattern until the end of the foundation chain. When you reach the end, make 1 dc in the last chain then ch 3 and turn.

Row 2: 1 dc in the first chain then skip 1 ch now 2 dc in the next ch and repeat this pattern until the you reach the last chain. Make 1 dc in the last ch then ch 3 and turn.

Repeat Row 2 until you reach 50 rows. If you want to make a shorter afghan stop when you reach the length you are happy with and fasten off.

Add fringe across the top and bottom of the afghan:

Cut yarn double the length of fringe you want, this blanket used 8 inch lengths. Now fold each length of yarn in half and with the folded loop first, pull it through the first chain. Now push the loose ends through the loop you just created and pull tight. Now you have fringe. Continue this process across the top and bottom of the blanket.

Chapter 3 – One Day Baby Afghan

Skills: Easy/Beginner

Materials: Crochet hook US size N or 10 mm, about 6 skeins or balls of super bulky or super chunky yarn, and scissors

Notes: Completed Afghan is about 33" across each side, the exact size will depend on your preference

Pattern:

Ch 50

Row 1: 1 sc in the 2nd ch from the hook, then *ch 1 and skip the next ch, then 1 sc in the next ch* now repeat from *to* until you reach the end of the chain and turn

Row 2: Ch 1 then 1 sc in the first sc and 1 sc in next ch, now *Ch 1 and skip the next sc then 1 sc in next ch* now repeat from *to* and then 1 sc in the last ch and turn

Row 3: Ch 1 then 1 sc in the first sc and *Ch 1 then skip the next sc and then 1 sc in the next ch* now repeat from *to* then ch 1 and skip the next sc and 1 sc in the last sc and turn

Repeat row 2 and row 3 until the work measures 33" from the first row to the last row and do not fasten off

Edging:

Round 1: Ch 1 then sc 47 evenly around each side of the afghan now sc 3 in each corner and join with sl st in the first sc and then fasten off

Chapter 4 – One Day Lacey Afghan

Skills: Easy

Materials: One ball or skein of Chunky/Thick yarn, crochet hook US size L, yarn needle and scissors

Notes: Special Abbreviation and Stitch

2trcl- *[yo] twice and draw up a loop in the st then [yo and draw through 2 loops on the hook] twice then rep from * one more time and yo then draw the yarn through all 3 loops on the hook

Pattern

Ch 82.

Row 1: Sc in the 2nd ch from the hook and again in the next 2 ch then * ch 3 and skip the next 3 ch then sc in the next ch, now ch 3 and skip the next 2 ch then sc in the next ch now ch 3 and skip the next 3 ch and sc in the next 3 ch and repeat from * across and then turn

Row 2: Ch 4 and skip the first sc then tr 3 in the next sc and skip the next ch-3 sp. (2trcl, ch 3, 2trcl, ch 3, 2trcl) in the next ch-3 sp; one tr shell made. Now skip the next ch-3 sp and *skip the next sc then 5 tr in the next sc then skip the sc and the ch-3 sp, and tr shell in next ch-3 sp; rep from * to the last 3 sc; skip the next sc and 3 tr in the next sc and tr in the last sc then turn

Row 3: Ch 1 then sc in the next 3 tr, now * skip the next tr and [ch 3 and sc in the next ch-3 sp] twice then ch 3 and skip the next tr then sc in the next 3 tr now repeat from * across then sc the in the top of ch-4 and turn

Repeat Rows 2 and 3 - 14 times and then repeat Row 2 once more

Last Row: Ch 1 and sc in the first 3 tr then * skip the next tr then ch 3 and sc in the next ch-3 sp then ch 2 and sc in the next ch-3 sp now ch 3 and skip the next tr then sc in the next 3 tr; repeat from * across and work the last sc in the top of ch-4 then turn and do not fasten off, begin the edging

Edging

Rnd 1: Ch 1 then * (sc, ch 1 and sc) all in the first sc now sc in the next 2 sc and ** now 2 sc in the ch-3 sp and sc in the next sc then sc in the ch-2 sp and sc in the next sc then 2 sc in the ch-3 sp *** and sc in the next 3 sc now repeat from ** to the last 3 sc and end at *** then sc in the next 2 sc, (sc, ch 1 and sc) all in the last sc and turn so you can work down side edge; **** now work 3 sc over the tr at the edge and sc in the st at the end of the next row and repeat from **** to the next corner st and turn to work across the bottom edge. Continue to work in the same manner across the bottom and then on the next side edge now join with a sl st in the first sc.

Chapter 5 – One Skein Lapghan

Skills: Easy

Materials: 454 grams of yarn or 2 average skeins. Crochet hook US size L, a yarn needle and scissors

Notes: Special Abbreviations and Stitches

CL (Cluster Stitch) - [Yarn over and draw up a loop then yarn over and draw up 2 loops] twice, all in the specified stitch or space, then yarn over and draw the yarn through all 3 loops on the hook

FPdc (Front Post Double Crochet Stitch) – Yo and insert the hook from the front to the back and back to the front around the post of the indicated stitch and draw up the yarn through and then [yarn over and draw through 2 loops on the hook] two times

BPdc (Back Post Double Crochet Stitch) – Yo and insert the hook from the back to the front and back around the post of the indicated stitch and draw the yarn through then [yarn over and draw through 2 loops on the hook] two times

This Lapghan measures 32"x37" when complete

Pattern

Ch 83.

Row 1 (Wrong Side): (CL, ch 2 and CL) all in the 5th ch from the hook then skip the next ch and dc in the next ch then * skip the next ch and (CL, ch 2 and CL) all in the next ch and skip the next ch now dc in the next ch and repeat from *across and turn, you should now have 20 cluster groups

Row 2 (Right Side): Ch 3 and (CL, ch 2 and CL) all in the next ch-2 space then * FPdc around the next dc and (CL, ch 2 and CL) all in the next ch-2 space now repeat from * to the last st and dc in the top of the beginning ch and turn

Row 3: Ch 3 and (CL, ch 2 and CL) all in the next ch-2 space then *BPdc around the next st and (CL, ch 2 and CL) all in the next ch-2space then repeat from * to the last st and then dc in the top of the ch-3 and turn

Rows 4-49: Repeat Rows 2 and 3 (23) times

Border

Rnd 1: Ch 1 and sc evenly around all 4 sides then work 3 sc in each corner and join with a slip st in the first sc

Rnd 2: Ch 1 and working left to right, sc in each sc around and join with a sl st then fasten off and weave in the ends

Chapter 6 – Fast and Easy Openwork Afghan

Skills: Easy

Materials: 2 skeins of sport weight or baby weight yarn, crochet hook US size P, yarn needle and scissors

Notes: Finished afghan measures about 50"x64"

Pattern

Ch 78.

Row 1 (Right Side): Sc in the 2nd ch from the hook and in each ch across then turn

Row 2: Ch 1 then sc in every sc across and turn

Row 3: Ch 1 then sc in the first sc and * ch 2, skip the next sc and dc in the next sc then ch 2 and skip the next sc now sc in the next sc and repeat from * across to the end and turn

Row 4: Ch 4 (this counts as dc and ch 1) then sc in the first dc and * ch 1 then dc in the next sc ** then ch 1 and sc in the next dc then repeat from * across and end at ** and turn

Row 5: Ch 1 and * sc in the dc then sc in the sp and sc in the sc then sc in the sp and repeat from *to the last st then sc in the 3rd ch of the ch-4 and turn

Row 6: Ch 1 then sc in every st across until the end and turn

Rep Rows 2-6 until the afghan reaches 61" from the beginning and end by repeating Row 6 one more time and do not fasten off

EDGING

Rnd 1 (Right Side): Ch 1 then 3 sc in the first sc and sc in every st up to the last sc and 3 sc in the last sc now sc evenly down the side edge. 3 sc at the corner and sc across the beginning edge then 3 sc in the corner then sc evenly up the long side and join with a sl st to the first sc and turn

Rnd 2: Ch 1 and sc in every sc around then work 3 sc in every corner sc and join with a sl st and turn

Rnd 3: * Ch 2 and sl st in every 2nd ch from the hook then skip the next sc and sl st in the next 2 sc and rep from * around and join then fasten off and weave in the ends

Chapter 7 – Sunshine Afghan

Skills: Easy

Material: 4 skeins of orange multi-color yarn, crochet hook US size K, yarn needle and scissors

Notes: This afghan measures about 52"x59" excluding the fringe. This afghan uses multi-color yarn instead different colored yarn and stripes like the image

Pattern

ch 183

Foundation Row 1 (Right Side): Dc in 4th ch from the hook then* hdc in next 2 ch and sc in the next 3 ch and hdc in next 2 ch ** then dc in next 3 ch and repeat from the * to the last 2 ch and end at ** and dc in the last 2 ch and turn

Foundation Row 2: Ch 1 then sc in the first 2 dc and * skip the next 3 sts then 7 tr in the next sc and skip the next 3 sts ** then sc in the next 3 dc and repeat from * to the last 2 sts and end at ** then sc in the next dc and sc in the top of the turning ch and turn

Row 1: Ch 2 and skip the first sc then dc in the next sc and in each st across then turn

Row 2: Ch 2 and 3 tr in the first dc then * skip the next 3 sts and sc in the next 3 sts then skip the next 3 sts ** now 7 tr in the next st and repeat from * to the last st and end at ** then (3 tr and dc) all in the top of the turning ch and turn

Row 3: Ch 2 then skip the first dc and dc in the next st and in each st across in the top of the turning ch and turn

Row 4: Ch 1 and sc in the first 2 dc then * skip next 3 sts and 7 tr in the next st then skip the next 3 sts ** and sc in the next 3 dc then repeat from * to the last 2 sts and end at ** now sc in the next dc and sc in the top of the turning ch and turn

Rows 5 and 6: Repeat Rows 1 and 2

Rows 7 and 8: Repeat Rows 3 and 4

Rows 9 and 10: Repeat Rows 1 and 2

Rows 11 and 12: Repeat Rows 3 and 4

Rep Rows 1-12 until the length is approximately 51½" from beginning to the end

Now work as follows:

Last Row: Ch4 then skip the first st and dc in the next st * and hdc in the next 2 dc then sc in the next 3 dc and hdc in the next 2 dc ** now dc in the next 3 dc and repeat from * to the last 2 sts and end at ** then dc in the last dc and dc in the top of the turning ch then fasten off

FINISHING

Fringe: Cut 12" lengths of yarn and knot 5 strands in each row as follows:

Fold 5 strands in half to form a loop then insert the hook from the wrong side of the fabric into the ch in the row and into the loop then draw the loop through the fabric and then pull the yarn ends through the loop and tighten and trim the ends

Chapter 8 – Puffy Tassel Lapghan

Skills: Easy

Materials: 11 skeins of sport weight yarn color of your choice, US crochet hook size J, yarn needle and scissors

Notes: This afghan measures about 40x50"

Special Stitch Used:

Popcorn – Pc: make 5 dc in the stitch indicated then drop the loop from the hook and insert it into the top of the first dc of the 5 dc group then put the loop back on the hook and pull through the dc

Reverse single chain – Rev sc: work from left to right and insert the hook in the next st to the right of the last st then yo and pull up a loop and yo again and pull through the 2 loops on the hook

Pattern

This afghan is created from crochet blocks similar to making a granny square blanket, you will need to make 20 of these blocks.

Ch 6 then join ends together with a slip st to form a ring

Rnd 1 (Right Side). Ch 3 (this counts as a dc) then 15 dc in the ring and join to the top of the beginning ch-3

Rnd 2: Ch 3 then [dc in the next 3 dc and (dc, ch 3 and dc) in the next dc] 3 times then dc in the next 3 dc and dc in the same ch as the joining ch and join with ch 2 then sc in the top of the beginning ch-3 (this will count as a ch-3 space here and throughout the rest of the pattern)

Rnd 3: Ch 3 then dc in the same st as the join st and dc in the next dc then * pc in the next dc and dc in the next 2 dc**now (dc, ch 3 and dc) in the next ch-3-space and dc in the next 2 dc then repeat from * 3 more times and end with the last repeat at ** now dc in the last ch-3 space and join with ch 2 then sc in the top of the beginning of the ch-3

Rnd 4: Ch 3 then dc in the same st as the join and * pc in the next dc then dc in the next 3 sts and pc in the next dc then dc in the next dc** now (dc, ch 3 and dc) in the next ch-3 space and dc in the next dc then repeat from * 3 more times and end at the last repeat ** then dc in the last ch-3 space and join with a ch 1 and hdc in the top of the beginning ch-3 (this counts as a ch-3 space here and throughout)

Note: The first popcorn stitch of Rounds 5–8 is worked in the same stitch as join.

Rnd 5: Ch 3 then dc around the post of the joining hdc then *[pc in next dc and dc in next 3 sts] two times then pc in the next dc** and (2 dc, ch 3 and 2 dc) in the next ch-3-space then repeat from * 3 more times and end the last repeat at ** then 2 dc in the last ch-3 space now join with ch 1 and hdc in the top of the beginning ch-3

Rnd 6: Ch 3 then dc around the post of the joining hdc and *[pc in next dc then dc in the next 3 sts] 3 times and pc in the next dc** now (2 dc, ch 3 and 2 dc) in the next ch-3-space and repeat from * 3 more times, ending the last repeat at ** then 2 dc in the last ch-3 space and join with ch 1 and hdc in the top of the beginning ch-3

Rnd 7: Ch 3 and dc around the post of the joining hdc then *[pc in next dc and dc in the next 3 sts] 4 times now pc in the next dc** and (2 dc, ch 3 and 2 dc) in the next ch-3-space then repeat from * 3 more times, ending the last repeat at ** then 2 dc in the last ch-3 space and join with ch 1 and hdc in the top of the beginning ch-3

Rnd 8: Ch 3 and dc around the post of the joining hdc then *[pc in the next dc and dc in the next 3 sts] 5 times now pc in the next dc** then (2 dc, ch 3 and 2 dc) in the next ch-3-space then repeat from * 3 more times, ending the last repeat at ** then 2 dc in the last ch-3 space and join with ch 1 then hdc in the top of the beginning ch-3

Rnd 9: Ch 3 and dc around the post of the joining hdc then dc in the same st as the join and *dc in each st across to the next ch-3 space** now (2 dc, ch 3 and 2 dc) in the next ch-3-space and repeat from * 3 more times, ending the last repeat at ** now 2 dc in the last ch-3 space and ch 3 now join with a sl st in the top of the beginning ch-3 spaces and fasten off

FINISHING:

Join the blocks into 4 rows with 5 blocks in each row as follows:

With the right sides of 2 blocks together, work through both blocks and join with a sc in each ch-3 space and a sc in each dc across each side to the next ch-3 space then sc in the next ch-3 space. Fasten off and continue to join the remaining blocks together working row by row and fastening off at the end of each row.

Border-Rnd 1: With the right side facing, join the yarn with a sc in the ch-3 space in any corner then sc in each st around edge and work 3 sc in every corner in the ch-3 spaces and sc in each joined ch-3 space and sc in each block joining then join with a sl st in the first sc

Border Rnd 2: Ch 1 and sc in the same st as the joining and work rev sc in each

remaining st around and join with a sl st in the first sc then fasten off and weave in the ends

Tassels

Make 4: Wrap the yarn around the cardboard 20 times and cut the end of the yarn. Insert a piece of yarn under wrapped yarn at top edge of the cardboard and make a knot. Cut the bottom edge of the wrapped yarn and remove from it from the cardboard. Wrap a piece of yarn around the wrapped yarn about 1" from the top edge and tie a knot and the secure ends. Trim the bottom edge evenly and attach 1 tassel to each corner of the afghan

Chapter 9 – Perfect Square Lapghan

Skills: Easy

Materials: Two skeins each of contrasting color yarn, crochet hook US size I

Notes: This pattern uses two colors of yarn instead of three like the picture shows, for pattern reading, make one color of yarn color A, and the other color B. This Lapghan measures approximately 39" square

Pattern

Using yarn A, ch 5 then join the ends with a sl st in the 5th ch from the hook to form a ring

Rnd 1 (Right Side): Ch 3 then 2 dc in the ring and ch 3 then [3 dc in ring and ch 3] 3 times then join with a sl st in the top of ch 3

Rnd 2: Sl st in the next 2 dc and into the ch-3 sp then ch 3 and (2 dc, ch 3 and 3 dc) all in the same ch-3 sp now ch 1 and * (3 dc, ch 3 and 3 dc) all in the next ch-3 sp and ch 1 then repeat from * around and join to the top of the ch-3 and fasten off

Rnd 3: With the right side facing, attach yarn color B in any corner ch-3 sp and ch 3 then (2 dc, ch 3 and 3 dc) all in the same ch-3 sp and ch 1 then * 3 dc in the next ch-1 sp and ch 1 then (3 dc, ch 3 and 3 dc) all in the next corner sp and ch 1 then repeat from * around and join

Rnd 4: Sl st in the next 2 dc and into the ch-3 sp then ch 3 and (2 dc, ch 3 and 3 dc) all in the same ch-3 sp then ch 1 and * 3 dc in the next ch 1 sp then ch 1 and repeat from * to the next ch-3 corner sp ** and (3 dc, ch 3 and 3 dc) all in the next corner sp then ch 1 and repeat from * around and end at ** then join

Rep Rnd 4 then work 2 more rnds with color B then fasten off

Next Rnd: ***With the right side facing, attach color A in any corner ch-3 sp then ch 3 and (2 dc, ch 3 and 3 dc) all in the same ch-3 sp then ch 1 and * 3 dc in the next ch-1 sp then ch 1 and repeat from * to the next ch-3 corner sp ** and (3 dc, ch 3 and 3 dc) all in the next corner sp then ch 1 and repeat from * around and end at ** then join now work 5 more rnds with color A then 4 rnds color B then 4 rnds color A now repeat from *** one more time then fasten off and weave in the ends.

Conclusion

All of the afghans should take only one day to complete if you are already familiar with crochet patterns and stitches. If you are new to crocheting afghans and reading patterns it may take you longer to complete them. With practice you will be able to do every afghan in this book quickly.

The patterns in this book are simple and look great all on their own, but you can spice them up with crochet appliques or sew initials onto them with yarn and a yarn needle. You can make them longer or shorter by adding or removing rows in the patterns or add boarders and fringe as you please.

When you finish all the afghans give them as gifts or keep them when the weather gets cold. The smaller size of the Lapghans make them perfect stroller blankets for baby or a soft cozy wrap for watching TV on a crisp fall night. They make great gifts for high school sports fans to, just alter the colors to match the school colors and you can even use them for fund raising; the uses are endless.

Crochet Sandals And Flip-Flops

Chapter 1 – Crochet Basics

Crochet is fundamentally a technique that uses a specific tool called a crochet hook that turns yarn – or fibers – into a textured or patterned fabric. The possibilities with crochet are endless and there are patterns and eBooks covering a range of patterns including, crochet for your home, baby or pet toys, stuffed animals or clothing. Beginners should start with simpler projects that involve crocheting in a square or circle to get a feel of the stitches before starting more intricate patterns ass it can be very easy to get lost. You will find easy, medium and hard patterns in chapters 2-9 to see you through each stage as you progress.

Benefits of Crochet

The benefits of crochet are numerous, some of which are surprising and many don't realise. Some include:

- Reducing depression
- Reducing anxiety
- Relaxation
- Stress relief
- learning a new skill
- Postponing age-related dementia
- Creating new and intriguing projects

Crochet can also be used for encouraging shy children or those with low self-esteem to be able to believe in themselves, as well as learn a new skill that can help with other areas of their lives in the future.

Before You Start

Here are some of the main points you need to bear in mind before you begin:

- Keep balls of yarn away from pets or animals to avoid them getting unwanted marks or pulling of the fiber which can damage the integrity of your project. Completed projects are less likely to fray, more durable and easier to wash so ensure that you protect your yarn or incomplete projects.

- Crochet hooks and needles should be kept away from children because they may seem blunt but can pose a health and safety risk.

- Keeping a clear workspace and an area to store your incomplete projects will not only protect them but will ensure that you don't slip or drop a stitch accidently or without realizing which could jeopardize your project.

It is also noteworthy to keep: scissors, a yarn needle and a stitch marker to hand, for your projects and these bare essentials will help you during your projects whether a pattern specifically calls for it or not.

If the yarn type is not indicated in the pattern then use Worsted Weight yarn as it is the most common, middle range fiber that is the preferred favourite for knitting and crochet projects.

Basic stitches & Terminology

Beginners should note that patterns can consist of written words or shorthand depending on the difficulty and each specific pattern. They are interchangeable and are written that way to make patterns easier to understand while ensuring they are not pages and pages long. You may find that some of the following patterns have a combination of both as it makes viewing the layout easier to follow over one or the other. This is something that as you progress, you will get used to and you may have already encountered this method before.

Shorthand:

Here are the most common shorthand for basic crochet patterns that you may encounter in the patterns in chapters 2-9:

- Single crochet (sc) – the most basic stitch that you should use unless it states otherwise.
- Stitch/stitches (st/sts)
- Slip stitch (sl st)
- Chain Stitch (ch)
- Chain 3 space (ch-3 space) – Any number could be used here depending on the pattern, they are interchangeable.
- Treble crochet (tc)
- Half treble (htr)
- Triple treble (ttr)
- Double crochet (dc)
- Half Double (hdc)
- Decreases appear as (dec or tog) – note that decreases can also appear specifically to stitches, for example Sc2tog also specifies single crocheting two stitches together creating a decrease.
- Round (Rnd) – this could also appear as "Row (Rw)"
- Repeat from * to * - repeat instructions inside the asterisk
- Repeat from ** to ** repeat the instructions inside the asterisk.

Additionally, it is useful to know that within these projects a new line could be referred to as a new row or round depending on the context but both are used interchangeably from project to project.

To Make a Slip Knot:

Before you start your project the first step is to secure the yarn to your crochet hook. It is important to note that within patterns this does NOT count as your first stitch and the patterns are based on the first stitch afterwards (unless it expressly tells you otherwise.)

Starting by pulling a strand of yarn from the ball is called the tail and when gently dropped over itself, 5-6 inches from the end it will form a loose loop.

Place the crochet hook inside this loop and pull it back through the front end with the hook. By gently pulling the tail, the loop will tighten around the hook and you are ready to start.

To Join Yarn:

Some of the following patterns involve using several colours which requires using a technique to join the yarn together. In order to do this without dropping stitches or ruining your pattern is by joining the yarn at the end of the row if you are able.

You can also use this technique on larger projects that involve multiple balls of wall.

The easiest way to do this is by working your original colour until you are left with two loops left on your crochet hook and then use the new ball or color to complete the stitches.

However, some patterns require you to change in the middle of the row. To do this you must have around 36 inches of the original yarn left and work together the end of the remaining stitches using a double crochet until your original yarn runs out and then you use your new yarn as mentioned above.

To Fasten Off:

This involves removing the yarn from your crochet hook and is usually done at the end of the project or at the end of each separate section of the pattern.

Making sure you fasten off ensures that your project and hard work will not unravel and you can do this by:

Cutting the yarn from the ball when you want to finish your project (ensuring you leave a 6 inch tail) and then using the hook to draw the tail through the last stitch and gently pulling tightly so that is does not undo.

Metric Conversions:

Crochet Hook & Knitting Needle Sizes

U.S. Hook	U.S. Needle	Metric	U.K.
	0	2.00 mm	14
B-1	1	2.25 mm	13
C-2	2	2.75 mm	12
		3.00 mm	11
D-3	3	3.25 mm	10
E-4	4	3.50 mm	
F-5	5	3.75 mm	9
G-6	6	4.00 mm	8
7	7	4.50 mm	7
H-8	8	5.00 mm	6
I-9	9	5.50 mm	5
J-10	10	6.00 mm	4
K-10.5	10.5	6.50 mm	3
		7.00 mm	2
		7.50 mm	1
L	11	8.00 mm	0
M, N*	13	9.00 mm	00

N, P*	15	10.00 mm	000
P*		11.50 mm	
	17	13.00 mm	0000
	19	15.00 mm	00000
Q		15.75 mm	
S	35	19.00 mm	

*There are some differences between U.S. manufacturers on these sizes

Chapter 2 – 0-6 months Baby Flower Motif Sandals

You will need

- Crochet Hook Size D-3
- Cotton Weight Yarn (soft) – 2 colors

Pattern Notes

- Size Newborn to 6 months 11cm toe-heel (approx.)
- Make pattern twice for pair

Pattern

For the Soles:

(Main Color) Chain 14

Round 1: 2 double crochet into 2nd ch from the hook, 1 double crochet into next 5 chains, 1 half treble crochet into next 5 chains, 2 half treble crochet into next chain, 3 half treble crochet into last chain.

Work back on other sides of ch – 2 half treble crochet in next chain, 1 half treble crochet into next 5 chains, 1 double crochet into next 5 chains, 2 double crochet into last chain and use a slip stitch to join in the top of the 1st double crochet (st count 31)

Round 2: Turn. Chain 3, 2 treble crochet into the base of the slip st, 1 treble crochet into next stitch, 2 treble crochet into next stitch, 1 treble crochet into next 9 stitches,

3 treble crochet into next stitch, 1 treble crochet into next stitch

Repeat * to * 4 times total

1 treble crochet into next 9 stitches, 2 treble crochet into next stitch, 1 treble crochet into last stitch and use a slip st to join into top of 1st chain-3 (stitch count 43)

Round 3: Turn, chain 3, 1 treble crochet into the base of the slip st, 1 treble crochet into next 17 stitches.

2 tr into next stitch, 1 tr into next stitch

Repeat * to * X 2 more.

2 treble crochet into next stitch, 1 tr into next 16 stitches, 2 tr into next stitch, 1 tr into last stitch and use a slip st to join into top of 1st chain-3 (stitch count 49)

Fasten it off.

For the Heels:

Round 4: Reverse side facing, from the centre treble crochet count 9 stitches on the right going towards the middle along the outer edge.

Join the yarn, chain 1 (do not count it as a st), 1 double crochet into next 19 stitches. (Stitch count 19)

Round 5: Turn. Chain 3, 1 treble crochet into next 18 stitches. (Stitch count 19)

Round 6: Turn. Chain 1, 1 treble crochet into next 2 stitches, slip st into next st,

1 treble crochet into next 2 stitches, slip st into next stitch

Repeat * to * to end (use a slip stitch into last stitch) – Stitch count 19 and fasten it off.

Round 7: (Have the outer heel facing you and join in new yarn color) Chain 1,

1 double crochet into next 2 stitches, slip st into next stitch

Repeat * to * to end (use a slip st into last stitch) – Stitch count 19 and fasten off.

For the Ankle Straps:

(Use 1st colour) Chain 20, slip st into 7th chain from the hook and slip st into each chain until you end. Fasten it off while leaving a long tail for sewing it on to the edges of the heels on either side.

The straps across the toe:

(Use 1st colour) Chain 15, do this twice to create 2.

Count 4 stitches along from heel edge on the sole and sew on either side. Now count 5 stitches apart and place the 2nd strap also on either side mirroring the 1st.

For the Flower:

Round 1: (Use 1st colour) create a magic ring. Chain 2, 6 double crochet into the ring and pull it closed tightly (leave a longer tail so that you can use it to sew onto the sandal)

Round 2: (use 2nd color) Chain 4, slip st into same stitch,

slip st into next stitch, chain 4, slip st into same stitch

Repeat * to * X 4 more

Slip st into next stitch, chain 4, slip st into 1st chain and close. Fasten it off, sewing the flower to the two straps.

Chapter 3 – Baby Daisy Sandals

You will need

- Cotton Weight Yarn
- Crochet Hook Size G

Pattern

For the Soles – (Make 4 of these per pair)

Round 1: chain 10 single crochet into 2nd chain from the hook, single crochet into next 7 chains (for the toe), 5 single crochet into last chain.

Work on the opposite sides of chains, single crochet into next 7 chains, 2 single crochet into last chain and use a slip st to join to the 1st single crochet.

Round 2: Chain 2 (count this as the 1st half double crochet) half double crochet into same stitch, half double crochet into next 7 stitches, 2 half double crochet into next 5 stitches, half double crochet into next 7 stitches, 2 half double crochet into last 2 stitches, use a slip stitch to join into the top of chain-2.

Round 3: Chain 2 half double crochet into 1st stitch, half double crochet into next 12 stitches, 2 half double crochet into last 2 stitches, join and fasten off.

The Toe Straps – (Create 2 per pair):

Round 1: Chain 13 and fasten it off

Allow a 6" tail so as to attach to the shoes.

For the Flowers:

(Using Yellow for the center) Chain 2

Round 1: 7 single crochet into 2nd chain from the hook and join.

Round 2: (Using white) Join the yarn and chain 5, single crochet into same stitch, *chain 5, single crochet into next stitch, chain 5, single crochet into next stitch*

Repeat * to * until 6 petals are created.

For last petal: Chain 5, slip stitch into next stitch, fasten it off and leave 6" tail to attach (7 petals total)

How to attach:

Straps:

Right-hand side (first strap) – From the sole center, count 7 stitches back and sew in the strap Sew the other end on the left hand side counting 11 stitches back from the center and sew again.

Right Hand side (second strap) – Counting back from the sole center 10 stitches and sew one end. Sew the other end on the left side counting back 8 stitches from the center.

Flowers:

Position the flowers in the center of the two sewn straps and use the tail to sew them both together (as shown in the picture) Fasten it off.

For the Heels:

Round 1: Counting 6 stitches back from second strap (on the right hand side) join white yarn and chain 2, half double crochet into same stitch and half double crochet into next 15 stitches.

Round 2: Chain 1, turn, 1 half double crochet into each st across.

Round 3: Chain 1, turn, 1 half double crochet across and fasten it off.

Ankle Strap:

(Right) - Chain 13, single crochet into 2nd chain from the hook. Chain 2, single crochet into next chain across and fasten off. Sew the other side of the strap to last half double crochet created on the right.

(Left) – Chain 13, single crochet into 2nd chain from the hook, chain 2, single crochet across and fasten off. Sew the other side into the left hand half double crochet stitches.

Buttons (make 2):

Chain 2, 5 single crochet into 2nd chain from the hook and join. Make sure to leave a 6" tail to use when sewing. Sew one on each sandal on opposite sides. (the right on the right and left on the left)

To finish:

Single crochet around the 2nd sole together to end.

Chapter 4 – Grecian Style Sandals

You will need

- Tapestry Needles
- Crochet Hook Size F
- Buttons (X 8)
- Worsted Weight Yarn
- Stitch Markers

Pattern Notes

- Suitable for 0-3 months
- Make 4 soles in total (two will be sown together)
- New abbreviation- Sc2tog = this refers to a single crochet decrease

Pattern

Chain 9.

Round 1: 3 single crochet into 2nd chain from the hook. Single crochet into next 3 chain, half double crochet into next chain, double crochet into next 2 chains, 7 double crochet into last chain.

Working on the other chain side: double crochet into next 2 chain, half double crochet into next chain, single crochet into next 3 chain (Stitch count 22) Use stitch markers and place here moving up each rnd.

Round 2: In the 1st single crochet, 2 single crochet into next 3 stitches. 7 single crochet, 2 single crochet into next 5 stitches, 7 single crochet (stitch count 30)

Round 3: *Single crochet, 2 single crochet into next stitch* X 3.

7 single crochet.

Single crochet, 2 single crochet into next stitch X 5

Single crochet 7, slip stitch and finish it off (stitch count 38)

Line up the 2 sole pieces and slip stitch through the loops on both soles all the way around using your 2nd color. (38 slip stitches)

Work through the slip stitches to find the middle heel stitch and count right 4 stitches to put your 1st stitch with a chain.

For the Body:

Single crochet into the same stitch, single crochet 9.

chain 15, slip stitch in 4th chain from the hook, slip stitch 11 downwards in the chain, single crochet into the next slip stitch onto the shoe Single crochet.

Repeat * to *around and single crochet 20.

Repeat * to * around and single crochet.

Repeat * to *around and single crochet 2. Do not tie it off but join it with a slip stitch instead.

For the Heel:

Starting where the slip stitch join is:

Round 1: Chain 1, Single crochet into same stitch, single crochet 7 and turn.

Round 2: Chain 1. Single crochet 2 together, single crochet 4, single crochet 2 together and turn.

Round 3: Chain 1. Single crochet 2 together, single crochet 2, single crochet 2 together.

Round 4: Chain 20, slip stitch into 2nd ch from the hook. Slip stitch 18, single crochet 4 (going along the top of heel)

Round 5: Chain 20. Slip stitch into 2nd chain from the hook. Slip stitch down the chain, slip stitch into 1st stitch on the heel and finish it off.

Chapter 5 – 0-3 months Bow Sandals

<u>You will need</u>

- Worsted Weight Soft Yarn
- Crochet Hook Size F

<u>Pattern</u>

<u>*For the Soles: - (Create 4 per pair and work in round)*</u>

Chain 9.

Round 1: 3 single crochet into 2nd chain from the hook. Single crochet into next 3 chains, half double crochet into next chain, double crochet into next 2 chains, 7 double crochet into last chain.

Work on the opposite side: double crochet into next 2 chains, half double crochet into next chain, single crochet into next 3 chains (stitch count 22) Add in stitch markers here and move up in each rnd to get a good seam.

Round 2: In the 1st single crochet: 2 single crochet into next 3 stitches, single crochet into 7 stitches, 2 single crochet into next 5 stitches, single crochet into next 7 stitches (stitch count 30)

Round 3: *Single crochet into next stitch, 2 single crochet into next stitch* X 3

Single crochet into next 7 stitches.

Single crochet into next stitch, 2 single crochet into next stitch X 5

Single crochet into next 7 stitches (stitch count 38)

Slip stitch into next stitch and finish it off.

(Using 2nd Color) Match the 2 soles together and slip stitch wrong ways together and tie it off. (38 slip stitches)

For the Body:

(Using 2nd Color)- Finding the center of the heel, move 4 stitches right and join the yarn. Make sure you work outside through the sl sts.

Chain 1, single crochet into same stitch, single crochet 17 and turn.

Chain 1. Single crochet into same stitch, single crochet 6 and turn X 8

Do not turn the last row but making sure you have 7 stitches each.

Single crochet 2 into same stitch (creating 3 stitches working in corner)

Turn the project 90 degrees.

Single crochet 7 through side sts down the strap top.

Slip stitch into next slip stitch on shoe.

Single crochet 20 and use a slip stitch to join but do not tie it off.

For the Heel:

Start at the joining slip stitch.

Round 1: Chain 1. Single crochet into same stitch, single crochet 8 and turn (Stitch count 9)

Round 2: Chain 1. Single crochet 2 together. Single crochet 5, single crochet 2 together and turn (stitch count 7)

Round 3: Chain 1. Single crochet into same stitch, single crochet 6 (stitch count 7)

Round 4: Chain 20. Slip stitch into 2nd ch from the hook, slip stitch 18, single crochet 6 (along the top of heel) Chain 20, slip stitch into 2nd chain from the hook. Slip stitch down the chain and slip stitch into 1st stitch on the heel.

Chapter 6 – Boys Open Toe Sandals

<u>You will need</u>

- Crochet Hook G-6
- Soft wool yarn – 2 main colors and 1 for the trim

<u>Pattern</u>

<u>*The 1st sole (using cream):*</u>

Chain 12

Rw 1: 3 single crochet into 2nd chain, single crochet x 6, half double crochet X 3, 7 half double crochet into last chain.

Finishing the rest of round in the back of chain: half double crochet X 3, 2 single crochet into 1st chain, slip stitch into 1st single crochet (stitch count 30)

Rw 2: Chain 1, Single crochet into same single crochet, 2 single crochet, single crochet X 6, half double crochet X 4, 2 half double crochet X 3, 3 half double crochet, 2 half double crochet X 3, half double crochet X 4, single crochet X 6, 2 single crochet, single crochet into same st as 1st sc, slip st into 1st sc (st count 41)

Rw 3: chain 2, 2 half double crochet into same single crochet, half double crochet, 2 half double crochet, half double crochet X 14, 2 half double crochet X 7, half double crochet X 14, 2 half double crochet, hdc, 2 half double crochet, slip st into 1st hdc and finish off (st count 52)

Work in the post of the stitches as opposed to the top which will give you an edging around the soles.

<u>For the Shoe:</u>

Using 2nd color (brown)

Count 5 sts and slip st into the post. Which will add the sandal aspect of the shoe.

Rw 1: Chain 3, 2 double crochet into same post, dc, 2 double crochet, chain 3, sk 5 posts, 2 double crochet into next post, double crochet, chain 3, sk 4 psts, 2 double crochet into next pst, double crochet, chain 6, sk 12 psts, double crochet into next pst, 2 double crochet, chain 3, sk 4 psts, double crochet into next pst, 2 double crochet, chain 3, sk 5 psts, 2 double crochet into next pst, double crochet, 2 double crochet.

Rw 2: chain 2 and turn. Half double crochet into next 15 sts/chains, single crochet 3 together (dec) (including last 2 double crochet on right and 1st chain along toes).

4 half double crochet in chain along toes, single crochet 3 together (including last chain from along toes and 1st 2 double crochet on left side)

Half double crochet into 15 sts and chain to end, chain 4, slip stitch into 1st half double crochet and finish off.

The left shoe:

(Count from slip stitch in rw 2) slip stitch into 11th st on right-hand side.

Chain 13

Rw 3: half double crochet into 5th chain (this will make the button-hole), half double crochet into next 7 chain, single crochet 3 together (including last chain and 1st 2 half double crochet in rw 2 after slip stitch), half double crochet X 20 (including 4 along the chain 4) and finish off.

The Right shoe.

(Count from slip stitch in rw 2) slip stitch into 15th st on left-hand side (count chain 4 as 4 sts)

Chain 13

Rw 3 (2nd shoe): half double crochet into 7 chain, single crochet 3 together (dec) (including last chain and 1st half double crochet in rw 2 after slip stitch), half double crochet X 20 (including 4 along the chain 4) and finish off.

For the trim:

(Using 1st color or introducing 3rd new color)

Single crochet along edge of toes and heel and weave ends through the soles.

Single crochet around top of shoes. Use single crochet 2 together decreases for the corners and 5 single crochets for the button hole chains, slip stitch and finish it off.

Now pull the ends through the bottom of sole to stick out underneath.

The 2nd sole:

(Using 2nd color)

Pull all ends through and add the 2nd sole.

Chain 12

Rw 1: 3 single crochet in 2nd chain, single crochet X 6, half double crochet X 3, 7 half double crochet into last chain.

Work rest of the rnd along back of ch.

Half double crochet X 3, single crochet X 6, 2 single crochet into 1st/last chain, slip stitch into 1st single crochet (st count 30)

Rw 2: Chain 1, single crochet into same single crochet, 2 single crochet, single crochet X 6, half double crochet X 4, 2 half double crochet X 3, 3 half double crochet, 2 half double crochet X 3, half double crochet X 4, single crochet X 6, 2 sc, sc into same st as 1st single crochet, slip stitch to the 1st single crochet (st count 41)

Rw 3: chain 2, 2 half double crochet into same single crochet, half double crochet, 2 half double crochet, half double crochet X 14, 2 hdc X 7, half double crochet X 14, 2 half double crochet, half double crochet, 2 half double crochet, slip stitch to the 1st half double crochet (st count 52)

Do not finish it off here. Add a second sole to strengthen the shoes by matching them up placing one on top of the other. Use a slip stitch to join together all around which will also act as a contrasting trim.

Chapter 7 – Beginner Barefoot Flower Sandals

You will need

- Crochet Hook Size I-9
- Worsted Weight Yarn (soft)

Pattern Notes

- Gauge: 18 stitches to 4"
- 0-6 months

Pattern

Chain 6,

Rw 1: single crochet into 2nd ch from the hook, single crochet across. Chain 7 and use a slip stitch to the 1st single crochet at the start of rw.

Rw 2: Chain 1, single crochet into each single crochet in the previous rw. Chain 7 and slip stitch into the 1st single crochet at the start of the rw. Chain 1 and turn.

Rw 3: Single crochet into each stitch across.

Heel Strap:

Chain 12 and join to the 1st single crochet onto the opposite sandal end. The loops should go from the sandal on both sides one to the other (but they shouldn't cross). Fasten off and weave in the ends.

For the flower pompom:

Chain 51,

Single crochet into the 2nd chain from the hook, single crochet into next 9 stitches, half double crochet into next 20 stitches, double crochet into next 20 stitches.

Edging:

Chain 1, skip the single crochet below chain 1 and reverse single crochet into the stitch before. Reverse single crochet all along. Keep a 24 inch tail ready for your needle and putting it together.

Sliding the needle and tail sew along the bottom of your flower and pull it tight as you work along to create the ruffle effect. Fasten the flower to the sandal top.

Chapter 8 – Pretty Petal Barefoot Sandals

You will need

- Cotton Worsted Weight Yarn (in 2 colors)
- Crochet Hook Size H

Pattern Notes

- The pattern is for one so make them twice for the pair.

Pattern

Create a magic ring.

Round 1: chain 1, 6 single crochet into ring and use a slip stitch to join and fasten it off.

Use a slip stitch to join the next color into any single crochet from the round before.

Round 2: (chain 3, 2 treble crochet, chain 3, slip stitch) within same st that was used for joining.

Chain 10 (loop for the toe) Slip stitch into same stitch

slip stitch into next stitch (chain 3, 2 treble crochet, chain 3, slip stitch) into same st

Repeat * to * X twice more, chain 25 (for the ankle, feel free to adjust to fit the right size) slip stitch into same stitch and repeat * to * X twice more and fasten it off.

This should create 6 petals and an ankle/toe loop. Weave together the ends to finish.

Chapter 9– Crochet Flower Flip Flops

You will need

- Worsted Cotton Weight yarn
- Crochet Hook Size D-3

Pattern Notes

- 0-6 months
- Make 4 soles per pair to reinforce

Pattern

For the Soles:

Round 1: chain 11, half double crochet into 3rd chain from the hook. Half double crochet into next 7 chains, 6 half double crochet into last chain.

Working on the opposite side: Half double crochet into next 7 chains, 5 half double crochet into last chain and use a slip stitch to join to the 1st half double crochet.

Round 2: Chain 1, half double crochet into next 8 chains, 2 half double crochet into next 5 stitches. Half double crochet into next 8 chains, 2 half double crochet into next 5 stitches and use a slip stitch to join in the 1st half double crochet.

Round 3: chain 1, half double crochet into next 8 chains,

(2 half double crochet into next stitch, 1 half double crochet into next stitch*

Repeat * to * X 5,

Half double crochet into next 8 chains,

2 half double crochet into next stitch, 1 half double crochet into next stitch

Repeat ** to ** X 5 and use a slip stitch to join into 1st half double crochet.

For the Straps:

Right strap: Chain 9, half double crochet into 2nd chain from the hook and each stitch across. 8 slip st into opposite sides of the chains and use a slip stich into the 1st half double crochet but don't fasten it off. Chain 4, single crochet in the 2nd chain from the hook and into next 2 stitches (Don't fasten off here either)

Left Strap: Chain 9, half double crochet into 2nd chain from the hook and each stitch along, slip stitch to the right strap. 8 slip stitch into opposite sides of the chains and slip stitch into the right strap, fasten off and finish

Join 2 soles together and use a single crochet all the way around both soles and then sew on the straps either side and in the middle to form the flip flop shape and fasten off.

For the flower:

Round 1: (In yellow for center) 7 single crochet into an adjustable ring and join

Round 2: (Join petal color) Chain 2, 2 half double crochet into same stitch,

slip stitch into next stitch and chain 2, 2 half double crochet into same stitch.

Repeat * to * around until you have created 7 petals and fasten it off but making sure to leave 6" tail to fasten to the sandals.

Final Notes and Advice

Yarn can be tricky to take care of and washing incorrectly can lead to your projects being damaged or ruined. Try to avoid machine washing where possible and hand wash or wipe down. That being said, it is understandable that these projects may see some extra wear and tear as they are being worn by babies and therefore you should make sure you follow these rules when machine washing:

- Never tumble dry
- Reshape when wet
- Keep the buttons fastened when washing
- Use non-biological washing powder and minimal softener or chemicals
- Wash at 40 degrees or below
- Do not place on a high spin cycle.

Following these steps will help to make your baby sandals last as long as possible.

Hopefully this eBook has given you some useful and fun projects to work on that you can be proud off and show off and they would make excellent baby shower gifts (especially in the summer). The patterns range from beginner to expert and you should be able to refer back to them time and time again as you progress.

Finally, enjoy your baby sandals and happy crocheting!

Wedding Crochet

Introduction

Each bride wants to feel special, as if she is the only thing that matters on her wedding day. A handmade crochet gown can turn that moment into a memory she can share for generations. Sure, you can run out and buy an expensive gown full of bling but it cannot compare to a handmade work of art created by a family member or even yourself.

No matter who the crochet artist is, the gown will be remembered and passed down to others who will cherish it. The important part of a crochet gown is the memories it creates and passes on. Each fitting is an intimate affair for family and friends. Nothing can compare to the family bonds and memories a crochet gown creates.

There are many items a bride needs to look her best on her wedding day. Some of these items may be perfect for the "something new" or "something blue" she needs. Creating the gown and accessories for the wedding allows you to work with the colors of the wedding theme and add a touch of style and flair to the plain white palate.

Of course the choice of yarn and yarn color is up to you but there are some considerations when preparing to create items for a wedding. Wedding gowns and items should be fine and delicate; try to choose yarns that are a softer or thinner than worsted yarn. These projects may be good for specialty yarns or thinner sport weight yarn.

Remember to choose yarns, fabrics, and accessories that can be cleaned. Some may need dry cleaning; others can be washed in a washer. Take note of any cleaning information included on the packages before you get rid of them.

You can add ruffles, fringe, or bling to any of the items you create. These crochet items are perfect for adding your own special touch. Charms, trinkets, beads, or pearls can be worked into the pattern as you go, or added later after the item is finished.

Take your time with each item you make. If you do not understand something look over the crochet abbreviation chart included in the first chapter. If you need more help, there are plenty of online videos to walk you through particular stitches.

If you are working with white yarn or light colored yarn such as off white or antique white, be sure to wash your hands frequently. Even hand you think are clean may leave marks on the yarn and discolor your project. It is a good idea to keep some hand wipes close while you work; there is nothing worse than finding dark spots on a white gown.

The gown in this book can be altered for use as a bridesmaid dress too. Just leave off several rows at the bottom until the desired length is reached. Use the color theme of the wedding to choose the color of the dresses. To complete the look, crochet matching clutch bags for each bridesmaid using the pattern in this book. The gloves too can be used for the bridesmaids, just use the theme colors and match the dresses.

The flowers used in the bouquet and boutonnieres can be used to create decorative centerpieces for the reception. The can also be used to decorate the seating for the ceremony. Just use the theme colors for the wedding and create as many as you need.

Another idea for the flower pattern in this book is to decorate a veil. Using the stitches from the wedding gown, crochet a rectangular stretch of fabric, stop the rows at the desired length for the veil. At the top of the rectangle, draw yarn through the pattern as if you are weaving, tie off one end and pull the other until it ruffles and shortens enough to be attached to a hair comb. Now place some of the crochet flowers randomly on the veil and its done.

With a little imagination, the patterns and projects in this book can be used for more than just the bride. They are easy to modify and the color choices in yarns are endless. You can make decorative items for the wedding in any color theme using the skills you will learn in this book.

Chapter 1 – Guide for Crochet Terms and Hooks

Before you begin, look over this chapter to familiarize yourself with the abbreviations used in this book. The abbreviations are standard crochet terms, if you do not know the stitches covered in the abbreviations, it is easy to find an online tutorial for beginners.

If you are already familiar with the stitches listed in the abbreviation chart, you will have no problem crocheting the patterns in this book. The patterns for each project use these abbreviations and hook sizes. If you are unfamiliar with these abbreviations, there are many good crochet stitch tutorials online to help you.

Crochet Abbreviations

beg – Beginning	bg - Block
cc – Contrast Color	ch – chain
dc – Double Crochet	dec – Decrease
dtr – Double Treble Crochet	hdc – Half Double Crochet
htr – Half Treble Crochet	inc – Increase
rep – Repeat	rnd – Round
sc – Single Crochet	sl st – Slip Stitch

sp(s) – Space(s)	st(s) – Stitch(s)
tog – Together	tr – Treble Crochet
tr tr – Treble Treble Crochet	WS – Wrong Side
yo – Yarn Over	RS – Right Side
( ) – Work instructions within the parentheses as many times as directed	* - Repeat instructions following the single asterisk as directed
** - Repeat the instructions within the asterisk as many times as directed	[ ] – Work instructions within the brackets as many times as instructed

Crochet Hook Sizes

U.S.	English	Metric
14	6	0.60
12	5	0.75
10	4	1.00
-	3	1.25
6	2.5	1.50

4	2	1.75
B	14	2.00
C	12	2.50
D	11	3.00
E	9	3.50
F	8	4.00
G	7	4.50
H	6	5.00
I	5	5.50
J	4	6.00
K	2	7.00
-	1/0	8.00
-	2/0	9.00
P	3/0	10.00

Chapter 2 – Crochet Wedding Dress

Crochet has always been a favorite with brides. Crochet openwork and lace are feminine and flatter all body shapes. This dress is made with "pineapple crochet", this type of crochet creates an openwork motif that is repeated. Pineapple crochet is a perfect stitch for a wedding dress because it is intricate and beautiful.

This dress requires a slip because the crochet work is open and lacey. For an antique or vintage look, choose a beige or off white yarn. This dress can be shortened by making less rows. A shorter version in a different color is perfect for bridesmaid dresses.

Skill Level: Intermediate

Materials: 100% acrylic yarn and hook size F

Note on Sizes: This pattern is for a small, sizes 8-10, the changes for medium 12-14 and large 16-18 are in parentheses.

Notes: This pattern is worked in two panels then sewn together at the end. Leave 7" opening when sewing together for the arm holes, and 7" slits on each side at the bottom.

Pattern: Work in multiples of 16 + 1

Lace Panel/ make 2

Ch 97 (113) (129)

Row 1: ch 1 then sc in the second ch from the hook and in every ch across. Now ch 3 and turn (beg. Shell made).

Row 2: dc 1, ch 1, then 2 dc in the turning ch, now *skip the next 3 sc, sc in the next sc, skip the next 3 sc, 7 dc in the next sc, then skip the next 3 sc.

Sc in the next sc, skip the next 3 sc, then 2 dc and ch1, now 2 dc in the next sc. (shell is made) * Now repeat * to * across and end with a shell in the last sc then turn.

Row 3: sl st and ch 1 in the center of the shell. Ch 3 and work the beg. Shell, [ch1, dc 1] in every dc, (7 dc) then ch 1 and shell in the next shell. Now rep from * to * and end with a shell in shell then turn.

Row 4: sl st and ch 1 in the center of the shell then ch 3 and work the beg. Shell, [ch1, dc 1] in every dc, (7 dc) then ch 1 and shell in the next shell. *ch 2 [sc then ch 3] in the next 5 ch – 1 sps, (5 ch and 3 sps). Sc in the last ch, 1 sp, 2 ch then shell in shell* Rep from * to * across then turn.

Row 5: shell in shell, then *ch3 [sc and ch 3] in the next 4 ch, - 3 sps, (4 ch and 3 sps), sc in the next ch – 3 sps now ch 3 and shell in shell* now repeat from * to * across then turn.

Row 6: shell in shell, then *ch 4 [sc, ch 3] in the next 3 ch - 3 sps, (3 ch-3 sps) and then sc in the next ch-3 sp, now ch 4, shell in shell* now repeat from * to * across and then turn.

Row 7: shell in shell, then *ch 5, [sc, ch 3] in the next 2 ch-3 sps, (2 ch-3 sps) and then sc in the next ch-3 sp and ch 5, shell in shell* now repeat from * to * across and then turn.

Row 8: shell in shell and then *ch 6, [sc, ch 3] in the 1st ch - 3 sp, (1 ch-3 sp) and then sc in the last ch - 3 sp, now ch 6 then shell in shell" now repeat from * to * across; turn.

Row 9: shell in shell then *ch 3, [trc, ch 3, trc] in the ch-3 sp, now ch 3, and shell in shell* then repeat from * to * across and then turn.

Row 10: shell in shell then *ch 1, sc in the next ch-3 sp then ch 1 and 7 dc in the next ch-3 sp now ch 1 and sc in next ch-3 sp, then ch 1 and shell in shell* now repeat from * to * across and then turn.

Now repeat rows 3-10 as a pattern. For a scalloped hem, end the pattern on row 8.

To add sleeves: Attach yarn in the sp on the seam under the arm and work the beg. Shell then ch 1 and shell in same sp now ch 1, [1 shell, ch 1, 1 shell, ch 1,] in each sp around the arm and join in the top of ch-3 of the beg. Shell, now sl st to the center of shell and work shell then ch 1, in each shell around and join as before. Continue working the pattern for the sleeve until you reach the desired length then finish off. Repeat the same pattern for the other arm.

Chapter 3 – Crochet Garter

This crochet garter can be the brides, "something blue", just use a blue ribbon or pale blue yarn. A crochet garter is the perfect accessory for a handmade crochet wedding dress. This garter is easy to create and it looks beautiful with the added ribbon accent.

Skill Level: Beginner

Materials: Crochet cotton size 10 white and blue. Crochet hook size 7, 3/8 wide ribbon in blue or white, enough for the circumference of the garter. Small ribbon roses in colors to match. ¼ "wide elastic and a needle and thread.

Stitch Pattern: Shell stitch. 2 dc, ch1 and 2dc in the stitch indicated in the instructions.

Row 1: ch 8 and shell in the 5th cha from the hook. Then ch 1 and skip 2 chs then shell in the first st of ch 9. Ch 4 then turn.

Row 2: shel in shell then ch 1 and shell in shell then ch 4 and turn. Now repeat this row until the garter is the desired length.

Finishing the garter: cut a 2 ½ inch piece of ribbon in half. Weave the ribbon through the chain spaces between the shells and then sew the ends together.

Weave the elastic through the shells under the ribbon and sew ends together.

Glue 2 short pieces of ribbon to center front of the garter then trim the ends off at an angle. Glue the ribbon roses on top of the short ribbon pieces.

Chapter 4 – Crochet Gloves

These fingerless white gloves are perfect and easy to make. This design looks great with a crochet wedding dress. Play around with yarns and needle sizes to create a style that is one of a kind or use the suggested materials in the pattern. When changing the needle or yarn types be sure to increase when necessary to make sure the gloves will fit; just keep measuring the glove against your hand as you go along.

The openwork crochet for these gloves is easy enough for an advanced beginner. The fingerless design makes it easy to hold glasses and any other item during the wedding without the item slipping from your hand. This style is timeless and can be worn after the wedding with any number of outfits that need a little vintage charm.

Skill Level: Intermediate

Materials: 50g of sport weight yarn in your choice of color. Hook size E.

Special Stitch: Pico stitch: ch 3 then 1 sc in the 3rd ch from the hook

DC-GROUP: 1 dc-group = in the same ch space work dc then work 2 dc and 1 ch then 2 dc. At the beginning of the round replace the 1st dc in dc-group with 3 ch.

Pattern:

Work in the round. Ch 50

Row 1: ch 1 then 1 sc in the 1st ch now * ch 5, skip ch 4 and 1 sc in the next ch * then repeat from * to * along the entire round now finish with ch 5 and 1 sl st in the 1st sc.

Row 2: Sl st until the 1st ch-space then ch 1 and 1 sc in the same ch-space now * ch 5 then 1 sc in the next ch-space * then repeat from *to* along the entire round and finish with ch 5 and 1 sl st in the 1st sc from the beginning of the round.

Repeat row 2 until piece the measures about 1½", then work **diagram A.1B**

Work 4 ch instead of 5 ch now work **diagram A.1B** until piece measures about 3"

Now using **diagram A.2**:

Row 1: Sl sts until the 1st ch space then ch 4 (this replaces 1st dc and 1st ch) now * 1 DC-GROUP in the next ch space then ch 1 and 1 dc in the next ch space and then ch 1 * now repeat from *to* along the entire round and finish off with 1 sl st in the 3rd ch from the beginning of the round.

Row 3: Sl st until the ch space on 1st dc group, now ch 4 (this replaces 1st dc and 1st ch) then * 1 dc group in the next dc and ch 1 then 1 dc in ch space on the next dc group and ch 1 * now repeat from *to* along the entire round and finish with 1 sl st in the 3rd ch from the beginning of the round.

Repeat Row 2 and 3 until the piece measures about 7" and Then work **diagram A.3** as follows:

Row 1: Sl st until the 1st ch space then ch 1 and 1 sc in the same ch space now * ch 3 then 1 sc in the next ch space * then repeat from *to* along the entire round and finish with 3 ch and 1 sl st in the 1st sc.

Row 2: Sl st until the 1st ch space and ch 1 then 1 sc in the same ch space now* ch 4 then 1 sc in the next ch space * then repeat from *to* along the entire round and finish with ch 4 and 1 sl st in the 1st sc.

Row 3: ch 1 in every ch space then work as follows: 2 sc in the ch space, 1 picot, then 2 sc in the same ch space and finish with 1 sl st in the 1st sc and fasten off.

Now use this pattern to complete another glove.

Diagram Key:

    Dash =   ch

    X =   sc

    A cross =   dc

    An Oval =   DC-GROUP: In same ch-space/dc work 2 dc, 1 ch and 2 dc

    The Arch =   PICOT: ch 3, 1 sc in 3rd ch from hook

    1 =   ROUND 1

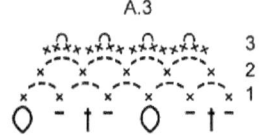

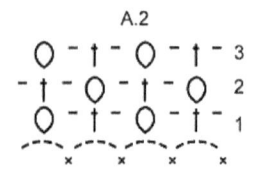

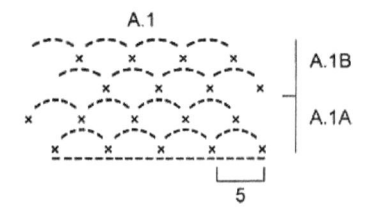

Chapter 5 – Forever Bridal Bouquet

This crochet bridal bouquet is beautiful. Because it is crochet you can keep it forever! You can even make matching boutonnieres for the men. This design can also be used for floral decorations and arrangements for the tables with a few adjustments. The color choice is yours, this pattern uses a pink and white theme, but this can be completed using any theme you wish.

Skill Level: Intermediate

Materials: Crochet thread size 10, choose 1 ball of each color you are going to use. Crochet hook size 3. A 6" Styrofoam ball and a 6" Styrofoam cone. Styrofoam safe spray paint in a color that matches the flowers or theme. Straight pins, pearl head straight pins, 20 yards of 1" wide double faced satin ribbon in a color that matches your theme or use antique white. A yarn needle.

Abbreviations Used: A for color A, B for color B, and C for color C. mm for millimeters.

Note: The flowers are worked using 2 strands of yarn held together for the entire project.

Pattern:

Rose:

Make 15 roses with colors A and B. With 2 strands of yarn held together ch 5 then sl st in the first ch to create a ring.

Row 1: ch 3 (this will be counted as a dc throughout) and then 11 dc in the ring. Now sl st in the top of the beginning ch and join.

Row 2: *ch 3 and skip the next dc then sl st in the next dc and repeat from *. Ch 3 and skip the las dc then sl st in the first ch.

Row 3: *(sc, hdc,3 dc, hdc and sc) in the next ch 3 space for the small petal, then repeat from * around the piece then sl st in the first st.

Row 4: Work behind the small petals and * ch 4, then sl st in the skipped dc on row 1 and repeat from the * around the entire piece the sl st in the first ch.

Row 5: *(sc, hdc, 5 dc, hdc and sc) in the next ch – 4 spaces for the large petal and repeat from * around the entire piece then sl st in the first st. Now finish off.

Carnation:

Make 17 carnations with color A and color B with 2 strands of thread held together then ch 18.

Row 1: 2 dc in the 4the ch from the hood and 3 dc in each of the ch across.

Row 2: *ch 3 then turn and sl st in the next dc and repeat from * to the end. Then finish off.

Leaf:

Make 12 with color c. With 2 strands of this color held together ch 10.

Row 1: sc in the 2nd ch from the hook then sc in the next 7 ch. Now sc 2 in the next ch and work along the opposite edge of the foundation ch, sc in the next 8 ch and sl st in the first sc.

Row 2: ch 1 then sc in the next sc and hdc in the next sc then dc in the next sc. Now tr in the next 2 sc and dc in the next sc, then hdc in the next sc. Sc in the next sc and 3 sc in the next sc, then sc in the sc and hdc in the next sc. Dc in the next sc and dc in the next sc now tr in each of the next 2 sc and dc in the next sc. Hdc in the next sc and sc in the next sc then sl st in the first sc and finish off then weave in the ends.

How to Assemble

Cut the Styrofoam ball in half and spray paint half of the ball, cover completely so this will blend with the flowers. Once the paint is dry, cut floral wire into 3" pieces and push them into the center of the crochet flowers and the edge of the crochet leaves to create stems.

Push the stems of the crochet flowers around the curved sides and the top of the spray painted Styrofoam ball and make sure it is covered completely. Arrange the leaves between the flowers and reinforce with straight pins if needed.

Pin one end of the ribbon at the center on the flat side of the spray painted foam Create loops around the edge and allow the loops to overlap and hang beyond the edge about 2". Now secure the loops with straight pins.

Using the pearl head straight pins, pin one end of the ribbon to the pointed end of the cone. Wrap the ribbon around the cone loosely creating overlapping edges so there is a tiered effect. Pin each wrap to secure and fold in any extra ribbon and loops and pin them.

Attach the handle (cone) to the bottom of the flower piece. Use straight pins and insert them at an angle from the cone into the flower piece, make sure they do not poke through anywhere.

The carnations are the boutonnieres for the groom and his groomsmen.

Chapter 6 – Beautiful Bridal Clutch

This bridal clutch is the perfect accessory for a crochet wedding gown. The clutch is lined and just the right size for holding bridal essentials. This sophisticated clutch is "something new" for the bride and a beautiful keepsake that can hold other keepsakes when the festivities are over.

Skill Level: Intermediate

Materials: one skein of yarn in your choice of color, crochet hook size G-6, yarn needle, and one set of snap fasteners. 8x14 inch piece of white satin for the lining, sew on silver charms for the front, a sewing needle and some white thread, and narrow, 12" silver ribbon.

Notes: This project is worked back and forth making a rectangle. The fabric lining is sewed on then the clutch is folded and seamed to finish it off. The finished size is 6 ½ x 8 inches.

Pattern:

Ch 44

Row 1: sc in the 2nd ch from the hook then *skip the next 2 chs and dc 5 in the next ch, now skip the next 2 chs and sc in the next ch. Repeat from * to * to end the row.

Row 2: ch 3 (this will count as the first dc) now turn. 2 dc in the first sc then * skip the next 2 dc and sc in the next dc, now skip the next 2 dc and dc 5 in the next sc. Repeat from * to the last 5 dc group then skip the next 2 dc and sc in the next dc then skip the next 2 dc and 3 dc in the last sc.

Row 3: ch 1 then turn, now sc in the first dc and * skip the next 2 dc then dc 5 in the next sc. Skip the next 2 dc and sc in the next dc. Now repeat from * to the end of the row finish in the top of the turning ch. Now finish off.

Assembly:

Weave in the ends on the crochet piece.

Lining: press ½" fold along the four sides of the fabric. Center the fabric onto the crochet piece and pin into place. Whipstitch the fabric to the crochet.

With the lined side of the bag facing up, fold the lower edge up 4" to create the body of the clutch. With the needle and thread, sew half of the snap on the lining side on the upper edge in the center. Fold the upper edge over to make a flap then lift the edge a bit and insert a pin to mark the placement for the other half of the snap. Now sew the other half of the snap where indicated.

Tie the ribbon into a bow and sew it along with the charms to the front of the clutch and it is complete.

Chapter 7 – Sweet Ring Bearer Pillow

Skill Level: Intermediate

Materials: 2 skeins of soft yarn, your choice of color. Crochet hook size H, a needle and thread, 24 pearl beads 6mm, 9 feet of 1-1\2" wide wired edged ribbon, 24" of 1\4" wide white satin ribbon, and stuffing.

Pattern:

Back of Pillow:

Row 1: ch 31, sc in 2nd ch from the hook then (dc next ch, sc next ch) across to the last ch then dc last ch and ch-1 then turn.

Row 2-24: (Sc next dc, dc next sc) across then ch 1 and turn. End row 24 and fasten off.

Front of Pillow:

Row 1: ch 5 then sc in the 2nd ch from the hook now dc in the next ch and sc in the next ch, dc in the last ch then ch 1 and turn.

Row 2-20: (Sc next dc, dc next sc) twice then ch 1 and turn. End row 20 and fasten off.

Make 12 of these strips

Lay 6 strips out and weave the other 6 strips over and under. Now take the strips with needle and thread to keep them in place.

The Edging:

Row 1: Lay both sides of the pillow together with the front sides facing each other now with an F hook work through both sides and join in any st then ch 1 and sc in the same st as beginning ch. sc in each st on the row working around (sc, ch-2, sc) in the corners now stuff before then close the pillow. sl st the top beginning with a sc then ch 1 and turn.

Row 2: Hdc each st around the pillow. Work (2 hdc, ch-2, 2 hdc) in each corner sp and sl st top beginning hdc then ch 3 and turn

Row 3: Dc each st around the pillow. Work (2 dc, ch-2, 2 dc) in each corner and sp then sl st top beginning ch 3 and turn.

Row 4: Ch 5 (1st trc + ch-1) then (sk next st, trc next st, ch-1) around the pillow. Work (trc, ch-2, trc) in each corner sp and end with a sl st in the 4th ch of beginning ch 5 then ch 1 and turn.

Row 5: Sc in each st and ch 1 sp around the pillow. Work (2 sc, ch-2, 2 sc) then in each corner sp then sl st top beginning sc then ch 2 and turn.

Row 6: Rep row 2 and at the end finish off.

Finishing the Pillow:

Sew a single pearl in each corner on the front of the pillow. Now sew four pearls in the center, one on each square. Cut the 1 ½" wide ribbon into four equal lengths then find the center of the edging on each side of the pillow. In the center edging on each side of the pillow begin weaving the ribbon. When the ribbon reaches the next center pull it through the front and tie it to the corresponding ribbon on the other side of the center. Tie each ribbon in a bow and add a pearl to the center of the bow. Now pull the ¼ inch wide ribbon through the corner to the center to hold the rings.

Conclusion

Every bride wants to look beautiful and crochet has always been an alternative for wedding attire and accessories. Vintage crochet patterns and dresses show that crochet has been in style for weddings since the first bride wore a crochet gown. With so many options for wedding gowns and accessories it is heartwarming to wear handmade items. Handmade items imbue each moment with love and a personal touch that cannot be rivaled.

If you are making some of these items for a loved one on her special day, you should know it will be treasured more because you have put your creativity and love into each stitch. She will know just how much you care and these memories will be passed down through the generations.

Each piece in this book can be used for other events too. Changing the color of the dress and shortening it by leaving off rows from the bottom creates a party dress or even a prom dress. The clutch can be done in different colors to coordinate with outfits in your wardrobe. The flowers used in the bouquet can be done in any color or theme and used to decorate any items that need a little style.

Caring for Your Crochet

Introduction

Do you enjoy crocheting gifts for people or making your own creations? Are you a beginner who is looking for more information on how to protect your projects? Then you have come to the right place. One of the best parts about creating projects is showing them off and using them year round. But yarn can be particularly fragile and easily start to degrade if it is not properly taken care of and the more you use your projects the shorter the life span can be.

In commercial creation the yarn undergoes chemical treatments and sometimes professional protection methods in order to extend its use and reduce it from being so delicate. However, many people do not have access to these methods or simply cannot afford them, so what do you do instead? This eBook will cover everything you need to know about hints, tips and ways to look after your crochet projects without breaking the bank.

First let's discuss when you know to take care of your projects…

Signs you need to care for your projects

The simple answer to this is that you should start caring for them from the outset and this will meant they are less likely to be damaged from the beginning. However this is no always the case and for gifts it may be a while before someone realizes anything is wrong. Some of the signs of damaged yarn include:

Fraying – When some of the edges begin to pull apart

Discoloration – Either darker due to dirt or grime or lighter due to sun or chemical damage.

Holes – This can be due to moths, catching or cutting the yarn accidentally

Causes itching – When your project causes itching or skin discomfort this can indicate a pest problem in your wool or yarn which is more commonly found in natural fibers than commercially bought. It can also be a sign that the project has come into contact with a chemical compound.

Unraveling – If any yarn has started to fray or disintegrate due to lack of care you may notice that the pattern has begun to unravel

Each of these signs need to be dealt with in a different way and may require you to do some fixing or re-crochet/weave in some more yarn to replace it. Hopefully you will take care of your projects before it gets to this point otherwise it may mean that it is ruined. All is not lost if you cannot salvage a particular project because you may be able to reuse the yarn or upcycle it which means to find a new purpose for it (for more information on this visit chapters 4 & 6)

Chapter 1 – Basic Washing Instructions

Yarn and wool which are the two most common fibers used in crochet and knitting can be particularly tricky to wash and take care of because of how fragile they are. If it is done incorrectly then all of your hard work on your project could be ruined by either miss-shaping, discoloration or shrinking which is why you should always follow any specific washing instructions that come with your wool. For example, recycled yarn, organic natural wool or yarn you make yourself generally has not undergone any treatments and needs to be dealt with correctly first to destroy any pests or bacteria that can linger. Those that haven't been chemically treated will not be suitable for sensitive skin without thoroughly washing first.

Hand Washing

Generally speaking, yarn or wool is hand washed to avoid damaging the yarn. For articles or projects that are quite long such as socks or scarves, hand washing avoids them becoming too stretched which can happen during the spin cycle in the machine (see below).

Hand washing is incredibly simple once you know how and all you need is:

- Lukewarm water
- Wool wash or specific hand wash detergent (to avoid aggravating your hands)
- Bucket/Sink
- Towels

Method:

1. Fill the bucket and add a ratio of 1 Tablespoon of detergent/wash to 1.5 Litres of water.

2. Mix it thoroughly until the detergent has diluted in the water.

3. Press your projects into the water so that the water seeps into all of the fibers in the yarn or wool.

4. Move the project article around in the water and make sure it is completely immersed in the water and leave it for 15-20 minutes to soak.

5. Drain the water out and rinse the detergent out thoroughly (with wool wash you don't have to rinse, follow the instructions that comes with it) alternating pressing some of the water out and rinsing again. Make sure not to wring or stretch out the yarn/wool or you could miss-shape it.

To Dry
1. Press out as much water as you can and place the article on a dry towel.

2. Roll up the towel and press down on it which will remove even more water.

3. Hang and air dry until they are ready to use again.

Hand washing doesn't always do the trick in today's modern times because there are more spills, messes and stains (especially projects relating to children or pets) that mean you must use a machine to try and disinfect or get a more cleaner finished project. Also, for regularly worn articles that may need more frequent washing you will find using a machine is easier and more time effective. =

7 Top Care Machine Tips

Here are some basic tips that you should know about cleaning your yarn that are a general guideline to start if you have nothing specific for your own skeins or wool stash.

No "vigorous" washing – This means ensure that you keep the spin cycle low and that you do not wring out the project after you have washed it. This is because yarn and wool tends to lose its slight elasticity when it is wet which means that when it is rung out or thrown in a high spin cycle it can become stretched and ruin the fit of your project.

Wash below 40 degrees – Avoid hot washes where possible because the heat can miss-shape the yarn as well as shrink your project. In addition to this on very hot washes it can even cause the wool or yarn to harden as if it were burnt which can cause scratching on the skin if worn.

Non-bio only – for those with sensitive skin, children and pets it is best to use non-biological washing powder which is softer on the skin and less likely to cause irritation or discomfort (especially on projects that have to be worn). This is because the biological components can sometimes linger in the fibers of the yarn and cause skin rashes or irritation for those who have frequent contact.

Re-Shape when wet – To avoid the wool or yarn from having kinks or losing its shape permanently, you should make sure that you gently re-shape the project before hanging to drip dry. You can use gravity to help straighten your project if you are hanging from a line (make sure not to damage the project with pegs/hooks)

Minimum Amount of Fabric softener – This qualifies for other chemical washing components as well that can not only linger and cause skin irritation in a similar way to the washing powder but the chemicals in fabric softener can react with any dyed wool or yarns which means there can be some discoloration or stripping your project of all of its colour.

Steam iron – Many believe that you can't iron yarn or wool as it can singe the edges and make them hard and coarse. However this is not the case, using an iron on a steam setting and spraying with water beforehand should protect your projects from the heat of an iron. Alternatively if you don't have a steam setting you can put the iron on a low heat and use a damp tea cloth or towel and iron through that to protect the fibers in the project.

No Tumble Drying – The best way to avoid damaging your projects (particularly shrinking or burning) is to avoid tumble drying altogether which can burn (and in some cases catch fire if left long enough) the project. If you decide to tumble dry anyway be wary of the static electricity and sparking risk after the cycle and avoid spraying any aerosols near the room when unloading the washing.

Fundamentally the key point to remember is to avoid heat on the yarn where possible which is the most likely cause of damage to projects.

Chapter 2– Stain Removal

Yarn or wool can stain easily, particularly if it is of a light color because it is easily absorbent and tends to hold the color in more (which is beneficial for the dying process but not if you drop food on yourself). The key to removing stains from yarn or wool is to try and do it quickly and as soon as possible. It is nearly impossible to remove certain old stains from the fibers because certain substances can permanently change the fiber color at a basic level if left over time.

The key to removing stains is to do so as quickly as possible, soak the article in lukewarm water as soon as you can after spilling to loosen the stain particles to avoid it causing permanent damage. The closer this happens to the time of stain the easier it will be to remove the stain.

Note: Dyed yarn or wool should be soaked only in cold water to avoid the colors from separating or running. In addition to this, if the color has a tendency to bleed or is unstable you can add salt to the water to soak it in at first to prevent too much bleeding. Always make sure to keep articles of separate colors in different soaks so that colours don't run or mix together which could ruin your projects.

Different Types of Stain Removal:

It is important to note that some of these methods may damage more sensitive yarns or may not work on all types of fiber but they are the better options for each of these types of stain:

<u>Wax (Including color wax)</u> – Freeze the article of clothing as soon as you can. Scrape off the excess wax gently (in some cases this is all that is needed however if there are remnants left use the following step) Using greaseproof or parchment paper either side of the wax, iron on a low heat to remove any excess. Wash and

rinse thoroughly. If the wax was colored and left a stain after removal, rub some alcohol using a sponge on the article and wash thoroughly again.

Grass - *This technique only works on light color yarns as it will strip the chemical dyes from darker colors* Alternate using ammonia and hydrogen peroxide on the stain until it is removed. Rinse with cold water and make sure to put it through a thorough wash so that all chemical traces are removed.

Food Stains - Soak in cooler water for an hour, use laundry detergent to gently scrub the fibers and then rinse with more cool water.

Lipstick – Spread petroleum jelly over the stain and leave for 30-60 minutes and then wash with warm soap water (making sure to thoroughly remove all of the petroleum jelly) and rinse with cool water.

Grease – Soak in warm water with soap or detergent and then use rubbing alcohol or light alcohol such as vodka on the stain directly. Rinse with cold water and wash thoroughly.

Blood – Soak in cooler water for an hour and then use warm water with mild soap or detergent to wash the stain thoroughly and then rinse with more cool water.

Chewing Gum – Place the article in the freezer overnight. Scrap off the gum in the morning and it should all come off easily. If there are still residues left in the fiber iron on a low heat between two sheets of greaseproof or parchment paper to transfer the residue.

Pet stains – Soak in warm water with detergent or soap. Roll the article between two towels and press firmly down on the stain so that the towel absorbs some of the moisture. Wash again in soap water and repeat until the stain is completely removed. Wash thoroughly

Tea/Coffee – Use warm water with soap or detergent to soak for at least 30 minutes and then carefully pour boiling water over the impact or stain points. Use cool water and the usual washing techniques after to remove soap.

Overall these are the best techniques found to remove the following substances from yarn or wool projects however some stains are impossible to deal with or could have been left for too long. If this is the case you may have to repurpose or recycle your project into something different to make use of the good leftover yarn.

Chapter 3 – Getting rid of smells

Sometimes your projects or articles of clothing that you have created will come into contact with lingering smells that you can't get rid of. Smells can sometimes be harder to remove than stains because they are all over the article and not confined to one particular area. Usually with normal cotton and fibers a hot wash tends to remove them completely without much problem however you are not able to do this with yarn because it is too delicate to be used with such heat.

Because of this there are special methods to removing certain types of smells from your clothing even if a particular stain is not apparent. The types of smells that can be removed are:

- Day-to-day smells – E.g. perfumes, household smells or plugins
- Body Odor – Make sure to pay particular attention to the areas it may be coming from for example the underarms.
- Smoke
- Pet Stains

Top Ways to Remove Smells

<u>Grass & Sunlight</u> – for those in sunnier climates you can use the natural UV rays combined with the chemical compound chlorophyll which is in the grass. This helps to renew articles that have been in cupboards for a long time and have the old odors such as mothballs or dust. Leave the article out on the grass on a very sunny day and turn every hour or so. It should be left outside all day and this should eliminate these smells.

<u>Charcoal (activated)</u> – Place the activated charcoal briquettes into an airtight container if your article is small or into an old sock or tights and place in a drawer with the article for a week and this should remove smoke or day-to-day smells.

This method works on many articles at once, increase the amount of charcoal being used for the amount of projects or articles being dealt with.

White Vinegar – Place the article in lukewarm water with equal parts of white vinegar and allow to soak for 10-15 minutes. Preferably use sunlight to dry the articles for the best possible results or alternatively drip dry. This shall remove pet stains, smoke stains and body odor smells.

Cat Litter – using clay cat litter (not clumping) can help to remove smells that also accompany wetter stains and are particularly useful for pet stains. Pour the litter into an airtight container with the article of clothing or project and leave for 3-4 days and the odor should be gone. Wash thoroughly before use.

Mint – Place fresh mint leaves into a bag or old pair of tights and leave in an airtight container with the article with odors for 2-3 days. Alternatively you can use Listerine or mint spray on the article to remove smoke smells (just ensure they have dried before wearing as this can cause skin irritation)

Baking Soda – Pour baking soda on your article in all of the areas that have the most odor. Leave in an airtight container or drawer for several days and then wash and rinse thoroughly. This is particularly useful for localized body odor smells e.g. under the arms.

Essential Oils – If you are aiming to quickly mask smells use essential oils dropped on the problem area and seal in an airtight container or zip lock bag overnight. In some cases doing this frequently will get rid of the underlying nasty odor permanently. Note: this method can be effective however removing essential oils from projects is nearly impossible so you will be unable to change the odor after it has been treated with one type of essential oil.

Lavender – Place fresh lavender stalks (with flower petals intact) into fabric pouches or an old pair of tights and leave them in the drawer or wardrobe to scent the yarn or wool and avoid old, stale smells. Change the bag frequently with fresh flowers. Note: this will also scent other fabrics as well so if you are trying to avoid this keep them in separate areas.

<u>Dryer Sheets</u> – Placing several dryer sheets into an airtight container with your article of clothing and leaving it in the sun for a prolonged period of time to get warm can help to draw smells out of the fabric.

<u>Multi-Washes</u> – See chapter 1 for techniques for washing however to remove certain smells, for example day-to-day or old musty smells from yarn or wool try hand washing or machine washing several times. Alternatively you can try stronger detergent.

It is important to note that these methods may not work and could damage more sensitive yarns and fibers. If this is the case it is better not to reuse these types of yarn/wool because the smell may linger in your next project.

Chapter 4– Renewing and repurposing old items and projects

You may find that your projects are no longer wearable or useable thanks to some stains or them becoming more fragile. If this is the case it is very common to re-use or recycle the projects so that the yarn is not wasted.

Even if a project has stains you can still repurpose for other projects such as pet toys (see below). However in some cases the yarn is not salvageable from a project because it is too worn and unstable and prone to tearing. Some signs to look out for when planning to recycle yarn are:

Thin fibers – This includes strands that are fraying so avoid these areas as they will not hold up to being re-crocheted or knitted.

Silky yarns – these tend to break and fray when re-used

Chenille yarn – these tend to shed and go bald when repurposed so should be avoided.

Signs of pests – reusing yarn that have potential infestations will simply transfer them from project to project and will not be suitable for re-use (especially if the new project is coming into contact with pets and children.

Smells- As mentioned in chapter 3, treat the project for smells before beginning to re-use it and if you cannot remove the smell you should not recycle the yarn as it is too embedded.

How to recycle yarn from an old project

Make sure to wash the project before doing anything else to ensure that it is as clean as possible because it is harder to wash the makeshift yarn balls or skeins that you will create.

Once you have determined that you have some yarn to salvage it is important to take a look at your project first and properly determine how you created it (or how it was created). For example, some seams you can cut along to aid the unraveling and some should be cut out altogether. You should pay attention to the different sections that were used to create the piece. For example, a jumper will have separate arms and two torso pieces formed together and you will be able to cut individual pieces off and unravel them separately which will avoid you getting things tangled. Smaller projects can actually be harder to re-cycle as there are a lot of breaks and you do not end up with much yarn at the end but do not be discouraged.

One of the key points to note when reusing yarn is that you should always wrap it as you go to avoid tangled, knots and breaking of the yarn. A ball winder is one of the easiest ways to efficiently do this and you can either purchase one or make one yourself by adding two nails to a board and winding around them. Wrap the yarn tightly to ensure that it will not unravel while being stored and pay particular attention to cotton yarn or other fibers that tend to fray as these will need to be wrapped tighter still.

Do not be alarmed if you have holes in your projects as this does not always mean that you have poor yarn, it could be that a stitch has come loose or been dropped which means that once you unravel it the yarn will still be useful and beneficial.

Ideas for leftover yarn

You may find that you have created a project and only have a small amount of yarn left after a re-use or repurposed project. It could also be that you only have a small amount of yarn available to after taking apart an old project due to stain or other parts of it not being viable. Either way there are some great ways to use small amounts of yarn for new and exciting projects that everyone will love and save you having to throw decent yarn away.

Pet Toys – Cats in particular can be really simple for making toys as you can knit or crochet small mice or pouches and put catnip in them to make a great toy. Also you can spruce up old jingly balls by making crochet covers for them and cats and small animals like to scratch at the yarn.

Dolls Clothes – If you don't have enough yarn for make a real jumper why not make one for your kids' dolls or teddies, they would love the imagination and you can have a fun new project. You could even use this to test out pattern ideas without using large amounts of yarn and doing it on a smaller scale.

Kids Toys – Crocheting and knitting opens up an array of stuffed toys or figures that you can make for kids. If you don't have children you could even donate them to children's' hospitals or charity shops to help out when you are done so that someone makes use of them.

Pompom's – These are small balls of wool that make great decoration for other projects, can be used as pet toys and also fun for arts and crafts for the kids. The joy of these is that you can just adapt the size of the pompom to suit however much yarn you have left.

Granny Squares – Turn your leftover yarn into a small granny square and eventually you can make a patchwork blanket or other interesting patchwork project from the leftovers. You can also use granny squares to patch up old projects or save the yarn for later when you might need them again.

Necklaces/bracelets – You can make really simple and elegant jewelry from the last strands of yarn that you have left simply by chaining (or knitting) to the desired length. This can be an interesting way to match fashion items with an inspired and handmade finishing touch.

Tassels – These are similar to pompoms but are actually a lot easier and involve simply tying the yarn together on itself. They are commonly used as adornments that you can attach to zips to help them to pull. They have also been used more recently as fashion statements and left on long pieces of yarn to make necklaces.

Pouches – These are fun and easy to create and again you can adapt the size of these to how much yarn you have leftover so they really are limitless. You will find that you can use small pouches to keep jewelry or other items or even some of your needles or supplies.

Chapter 5– FAQ's about yarn care

Here is a quick roundup of the most common questions that are asked about how to best care for your yarn or wool.

Can you wash an entire skein?

In some cases you may need to wash the skeins or yarn balls before use (spillages etc) and although this can be difficult it is possible. The trickiest part about this is to ensure that the yarn doesn't unravel which you can do by putting it in a pair of tights or washing bag beforehand. However, make sure to follow the same washing guidelines and check to see that all detergent has been rinsed out (you may need to hand rinse them to make sure as this could cause irritation if there is residue)

How often should you wash yarn or wool?

This depends on the amount of wear and the purpose of the project. For example a crochet bag may only need to be sponged down once in a while whereas clothes would need to be washed more frequently. Clothes such as socks would definitely need to be washed after each use to avoid any fungal or bacterial infections while a jumper may be worn a few times before needing to be washed. It entirely depends.

Can you dye your own yarn?

The answer to this is yes and the easiest types of yarn to dye are those that are animal fibers, for example alpaca, wool or mohair. Make sure to protect your skin and clothes when dying your own yarn as it easily transfers and can cause a large mess. For synthetic yarn you will need to buy specific dye to use for the fiber.

How do you find yarn care instructions for other yarn?

Usually, yarn will come with a wraparound label that has specific washing instructions on the outside or overleaf of the label. Some special types of yarn will come with packet instructions and others may not come with anything at all. The more specialised the yarn is, the more likely you are to get instructions. Generally speaking worsted weight yarn which is most commonly used is also more durable which means you are less likely to get specific instructions.

Can you get rid of old stains and smells?

Yes, however not always and a lot of dried on stains or lingering smells are hard to get rid of. The longer the stain or smell has been present on the fiber, the harder it is to get rid of.

Can you tumble dry?

It is best not to tumble dry yarn or wool as it is very sensitive to temperature and it can make it rough or coarse on the skin (as well as risk of shrinking) if it is exposed to higher temperatures. If you choose to use the tumble dryer it is best to do so on a cool or very low heat setting for short amounts at a time to check it is not having adverse effects on the fibers.

How long can you keep yarn or wool for?

Wool or yarn can be kept for a very long time over a range of years if it is stored properly in the right conditions and maintained. Wool that has been kept for over 10 years may not be viable for crocheting or knitting because it has started to degrade but this depends on the type. Organic fibers that haven't been treated may not last as long as store-bought that have been chemically treated.

How do you store yarn?

Store in skeins or balls in a dry place and make sure to clean out and check frequently to avoid your stash coming into contact with a lot of dust, moths or pests that might contaminate the supply. In addition avoid getting your stash wet and ensure that you frequently air it out to avoid there being a musty smell embedded in the yarn.

Conclusion

Hopefully this eBook will have given you all of the advice and help that you need to successfully look after your projects. You should have the right information to wash your yarn and make sure that it is regularly looked after. In addition you should be able to remove stains and smells effectively to avoid any permanent damage for all those accidents which means you can create projects for your pets or children worry free. Lastly you should be able to now repurpose or re-use your projects effectively to avoid them going to waste and make them last even longer. Finally this eBook should have been able to provide the answers that you need for any of the last minute questions you have about yarn or wool care. Good luck caring for your future projects.

Making Money with Your Crochet

Introduction

Crochet never goes out of style; even when it is not in fashion, afghans, baby blankets, scarfs, and hats are still sought after. New parents always hope someone crochets a blanket or bunting for their new arrival. The internet has made it easy for family and friends who don't crochet, to purchase adorable blankets and other baby items without learning to crochet themselves.

Let's face it, crochet is a skill and an art form, most people can learn to crochet, but not everyone can crochet well. Your skill and artistic abilities are in demand, you just have to learn how to put it all together and start making some money. You are about to learn everything you need to know about crocheting for profit.

There is competition in every business and selling crocheted items is no exception. Start thinking about what makes your crochet different from the rest; is there something you like to add that gives your items a unique flair? Do you excel at making flowers or granny squares? It will give you a competitive edge if you can come up with a unique angle for marketing your skill. Chapter 2 is going to take you from coming up with a name for your business to using a bit of marketing to bring in the customers.

When you decide what items to include in your inventory, ask friends and family what they think. Friends and family know your talent better than you do and they can be an invaluable source of inspiration and support. Include them when you make decisions about the items you want to sell, or the colors you want to use. Remember, customers have different tastes in what they like, don't worry about stepping out of your comfort zone, your family and friends may just spice up your items and set you up for more profit.

When you are surfing around the internet, do searches for anything related to crochet. Take note of topics bloggers are blogging about and stay up to date on the newest fads in crochet. You may not want to make fad items, but they may inspire you to create something similar and start your own fad.

Unique and one of a kind can spark a buyer to learn more about the item they are interested in. Many people love to know they own something no one else has. Adding a few one of a kind items to your repertoire can help you boost profits and repeat customers.

If you think starting your own crochet business is too much for you to handle, you are wrong. Gone are the days of huge overhead and complicated store management. You can actually open a store using Google web hosting and they will provide you with marketing analytics that will help you compete in the niche you are in. Facebook too has page analytics that will help you track visitors to your page and give you insight into which posts generate interest and which ones don't!

It couldn't be easier or more profitable to start your own online business, selling your own crochet items. There is little to no overhead, only the fee you pay for web hosting or selling, and the money you spend to purchase supplies. You can even find wholesale pricing on the crocheting supplies you need to make the items you want to sell.

This is not a business your grandparents would recognize; your crochet business has the potential to sell globally. No one is limited in where they can sell and the global market place is clamoring for more awesome crochet items. You might as well meet that demand and start selling your crochet items today!

Chapter 1 – Where to Sell Your Crochet

There are many places to sell your crochet; choosing the right selling outlet for your crochet depends on what you want to sell. Some crocheters prefer to sell one-off items instead of offering several different items. Others prefer to set up an online store and sell many items. This chapter will cover the different outlets for your crochet.

Craft Fairs & Shows
Craft fairs and craft shows are a great place to sell your crochet items. This type of outlet is a great choice if you have enough stock to set up a stand. Crocheters who sell at fairs and shows usually have several different items to offer; they spend the off season crocheting their stock and getting ready for show season.

If you want to sell your items but you don't want to manage a store, selling at fairs and shows may be for you. Do a little research in your area to find the fairs and shows that are close enough for you to travel to. Churches, schools, local clubs, fire stations, and community centers are a few of the organizations that hold craft fairs and shows.

Once you find the fairs and shows you are interested in attending, you pay for a table/stall/stand in the fair or show. Once you pay you are guaranteed a space and you will be informed of how much room you will have, or how many tables. Some shows provide tables, other make you bring your own, the organization holding the fair or show will provide you with all the information you will need.

Set your prices according the time you spent making your items, and include the materials you used. Do a search online to get an idea of what others are charging for the same type of items; this will help you set your prices and keep you competitive. You can even go to a few fairs and shows to check out the competition before you join in.

You can make your own tags for your items and include the price. There are many sites on the internet where you can create your own tags and print them out. If you are extra crafty you can create your own with stamps, inks, or any other media you want.

After you have tagged your items, choose a representative from each item you are selling and display it at your stand so customers can see the merchandise. The rest of your stock should be bagged so it stays clean and fresh during set up and transit. There are many different sized plastic bags you can use, you can find these bags at craft stores, online, or in your local supermarket. Bag every item you make and make sure your tags are clearly visible.

You can use your crafting skills to make your stand eye-catching and bring in customers. Use your display items to decorate your space, use a quilt stand to display afghans or baby blankets, and create a sign for yourself. If you plan to go to more than one fair or show, create a name for yourself and your merchandise so customers will remember where they got that awesome crochet headband! Make business cards for your stand too, and be sure to place one in every bag.

Here is a list of top selling crochet items at craft fairs and shows:

- Crochet headbands & ear warmers
- Crochet cowls and scarfs
- Baby items
- Boot cuffs
- Pot holders
- Dish towels and dish cloths
- Shawls

- Slippers and socks
- Character hats

This list is not the be all end all of selling at shows and fairs, but these items sell quickly and will give you a decent profit margin. If you have created a pattern for something unique, this is the place to sell it! Those who frequent craft fairs and shows are always on the lookout for unique items that they haven't seen before.

Online Market Places

Amazon, Etsy, and eBay are three of the most popular online market places. Using an online market place to sell your crochet items is easy, time saving, and cost effective. One of the best things about selling on one of these sites is the ability to see what others are charging and what items are selling the best. A simple search for the top sellers in "crochet" will give you an idea of what to sell and what to charge.

eBay uses a seller reputation system to provide consumers with feedback about the seller they plan to buy from. Your reputation on eBay is important if you want to establish a customer base, the better your reputation, the more customers will trust you and the more money you will make.

On eBay you will need a seller name, and you will have the option to fill out a page about yourself and your items. This is where you begin to establish your reputation. Fill out these pages to give consumers an idea of who they are dealing with, this builds trust. Express your passion about crochet, let potential customers know you love what you do and that you are knowledgeable about the items you sell. When you do sell an item, always leave feedback, this will prompt your customers to do the same.

When selling on eBay, always use pictures of your items. Learn how to take the best pictures you can, it is possible to take excellent pictures with your smart phone. Check out some "how to" sites on the internet on how to take product pictures. Many sites will walk you through everything you need to know, from lighting to editing. Remember, the better the picture, the easier it is to sell.

eBay is an auction site, it gives you the option to sell to the highest bidder, or set a "buy now" option. Many people like to bid, and just as many prefer to buy it now. Choose whichever you are comfortable with. Bidding takes longer to sell an item because consumers are given time to bid against each other. The buy it now option is just what it says, buy it now.

If you decide to sell on eBay, you will need to create some selling policies and these will be listed with your item. You will need to clearly state your return policy or no returns, and give a time limit. When you set up your seller profile, you will choose payment methods to accept. PayPal is one payment that is accepted all over the internet, PayPal makes it easy to accept all types of payments from customers. You will also have to choose shipping methods, eBay explains all about shipping, seller policies, and payment types when you sign up.

Amazon is similar to eBay but they have different policies and rules for sellers to adhere to. When you sell on Amazon, customers will give reviews of your items and you as a seller. These reviews will help you gain trust with consumers and make selling your items easier. Rules for selling on Amazon and similar sites change from time to time so it is best to go to the site and read through their rules and guidelines.

Again, any market place site you choose to sell on will require pictures of your items, seller policies for returns and refunds (some sites require you to adhere to their return and refund policies), shipping methods (the site will guide you through this), payment methods, and seller profiles (most sites have this feature).

Items that are popular on market place sites change from time to time. Always do a search for "top sellers" or "best sellers", this will give you an idea of what is selling and how much it is selling for. When you sell at an online market place, you will be charged a fee; this varies depending on the site, it is usually a percentage of your item price, and some will charge an upfront flat fee.

Open Your Own Online Store

If you are a prolific crocheter and have enough items to sell, opening your own online store may be the best choice for you. If you open your own store, you set the rules and policies. Opening your own store is actually easy and cost effective. Running an online store is similar to a brick and mortar business but the overhead is way cheaper and you don't have to hire employees!

There are many ecommerce building businesses who specialize in creating web sites for stores. Some companies offer the tools to build your own site and then charge a monthly fee. These companies have different skills they offer for a fee; some will even generate customer for your web store!

Here is a list of web sites that offer web hosting/building and marketing

- Shopify
- Volusion
- Square Space
- Wix
- 3Dcart

There are many more ecommerce builders, the main difference is in what they offer and how much the charge. Most ecommerce builders charge monthly for the online store; prices vary but they all have affordable options. Some even have tools for tracking your sales, projecting profits, and other ecommerce tools.

This is a list of things you will need when you decide to open an online store

- A logo (something customers will remember, important for marketing)
- Stock (this is always a good idea when you open a store!)

- A marketing plan

- An easy to use and maintain online storefront/store

- Well defined and clearly stated store policies

- Pictures of your products

Another excellent idea for your store is a blog. Customers today love to read blogs about the items they are interested in purchasing. If you don't write, it is worth finding a writer to do this for you. A "crochet" blog will help you generate sales and keep customers coming back. Use the blog to introduce your products, your passion, and throw in a few free crochet patterns; cover topics that are interesting to you as a crochet artist and they will be interesting to those who buy crochet items too.

Chapter 2 – How to Manage Your Crochet Business

This chapter is all about managing your crochet business. Everything covered here is important to making money with your crochet items. Of course you will customize everything to suit your personal vision, but all of these topics are a must for running your business effectively and generating a profit.

Marketing:
Marketing is one of the most important things you will tackle when it comes to running your own business. There are many companies out there who will do this for you for a fee, but doing it yourself is not as difficult as it seems. Most business rely on email marketing to inform customers of sales and to just keep the business in the minds of potential consumers.

Email may be a mainstay for most online businesses but it is not the only way to market effectively. Blogging was mentioned in chapter one as an important way to generate sales and it is one of the best ways to attract potential customers. Using email and a blog together is very effective. Most people will provide their email to receive blog updates quicker than they will to receive personalized commercials in their inbox.

Make an awesome logo! Your logo will announce your presence to the world so make it memorable. Use the name of your store in your logo, incorporate the initials, or create an image that stands for the name of your store. Use your imagination and you will come up with something great; you can always hire someone to create a logo for you, but you are a creative person, go ahead and give it a try. Do an online search for crochet stores and check out their logos, this is a good way to get a feel for making one of your own.

Social media is one of the best ways to generate business. Facebook has the option to create a page for your business. Use the page on Facebook to tell your followers about your newest product, drop interesting information about your blog, and post relevant "crochet" posts to keep your followers interested in crochet and your business.

There are so many ways to use social media to promote your new store. For every friend or family member you recruit to follow your page, there is the potential to generate more followers. Offer discounts for following you, offer free crochet patterns from time to time, and create a short video on YouTube on "how to crochet" basics; all of these things can and do generate traffic to your site.

Maintain a twitter account and use it to spread the word about your awesome store by posting links to your "how to videos", free patterns, and discount offers.

Make sure you choose something interesting from your blog and tweet a few lines to get people interested in following the link to your store.

Special Orders:
Special orders are not as profitable as the small easy to craft items. Generally special orders require certain colors, types of yarn, and size requests. Customers do like the option for a special order if they cannot find the size or color they want, but it can be time consuming for you as well. It is a good idea to add a fee for special orders if you decide to offer them. This is something you will have to decide for yourself.

Special orders are attractive to those who are looking for customized items for babies, or specific events. Monograming is one special order that is easy to do and is not time consuming. The choice is yours, if you do decide to offer special orders, be sure to include a section in your store policies about these orders. It may be hard to resell an item with initials or odd colors; offer returns at your discretion.

Store Policies:
Store policies let your customers know exactly what to expect when they purchase an item from you. You need to explain returns, refunds, exchanges, shipping, *special orders, and discount offers. Look at the store polices on sites you visit; this will give you an idea on what to include in your store policies.

Accepting Payments:
When you create your online store, you will have a *shopping cart*. Customers will add items to their shopping cart and when they are finished they will check out. You will need to provide your customers with payment methods to complete the checkout process. PayPal is one way to offer customers the ability to pay with their own credit card or debit card through PayPal. There are many other online payment options to choose from. Research online payment methods and choose the one that provides what you are looking for. Some charge you a fee for using their service to accept different types of payment methods, all of the rules are spelled out when you read through their policy agreements.

Taxes:

When you open an online store you will need to make sure you handle your own taxes. The best thing to do is to find and purchase tax software for the self-employed, quicken by Quick Books provides this type of software. Using tax software to keep track of your taxes is the best way to stay out of trouble with the IRS.

Shipping:

You have several options for shipping items to your customers. You can use the post office, or a privately owned shipping company like FedEx, or UPS. The fees associated with your choice of shipping should be listed in your store policies. Include a handling fee to cover the cost of packaging and allow your customers to calculate shipping when they check out. Another popular way to handle shipping is to just add it to the price of your item and state that shipping is included; this only works if you use flat rate shipping methods.

How to Price Your Items:

Pricing your items for sale can seem challenging. You spent a lot of time creating your items, and the price you paid for your supplies should be worked in…you don't want to over price, and underpricing will have you working your butt off for less than others are charging. There is a formula that will help you price your items, make a profit, and have return customers.

Market research is the first step. You must do some research online at stores similar to the one you are opening, or on the market place where you plan to sell your items, or at craft shows and fairs where you want to have a table or stall. Once you have an idea of what others are charging for similar items, you need to find out if those items sell for the price they wanted.

If someone is selling similar scarfs to yours on eBay and they charge $35 that does not mean they actually sell if for $35. You need to see what they have sold in order to know what they get for a scarf. After you know what your competition is selling their items for, you know the price rage for your own. Try to sell right in the middle or just a bit under the average price, then slowly up your price as you gain repeat customers.

Chapter 3 – How to Use Pinterest and Etsy to Sell Your Crochet

Pinterest and Etsy are a great combination for selling your beautiful crochet items. If you don't already know, Pinterest is a web site that provides people with the ability to search and save "Pins" of things they like, want, need, love…people save pins for all sorts of reasons. These "Pins" are saved to a board of similar pins about the same subject.

For instance, if you joined Pinterest and you love crochet, you might create a board called "I love Crochet", you would then do searches and find "crochet" items you want to save and remember. Pinterest is an awesome place to market your crochet items.

The more interesting your pins are to other people, the more people will "follow" your board. Now you have potential customers following your crochet board, and they want to see what you have made, they are interested in your products and now you need a place to host your "store" so you can sell them the items they want; this is where Etsy comes in.

Etsy is a community of creative people who sell their handmade items. People shop at Etsy to purchase items that crafters make, and crochet is a big seller. All you have to do is open an Etsy store and pin the items you make onto Pinterest for your followers to see…and purchase!

Etsy is unique because it caters to crafters and artists, other online market places are diverse with thousands of sellers selling everything from sneakers to handmade barrettes. Etsy is different, all of the sellers are crafters and artists, and now they have a unique place to sell their items.

Pinterest is unique because it does the research for you, you don't have to research marketing details when you use a site like Pinterest. The individuals who are following your boards are interested in your items, they want to see your stuff and purchase from you. Etsy and Pinterest are a perfect combination.

All you have to do to use Pinterest is sign up with a valid email address. Then you create boards and start pinning, it couldn't be easier! When you sign up for Etsy, the site will guide you through everything you need to do to get your store up and running. Etsy charges a minimal fee and the perks are well worth the price.

Etsy provides space for you to explain your craft and share your passion for what you do. Make sure you use the option to share your vision for your crochet work, and involve your potential customers in your love of crochet. The more information you give, the more people want to read it.

Etsy and Pinterest work together seamlessly but you can use any online store, outlet, or marketplace and use Pinterest as a serious marketing tool. When you have followers you have a readymade customer base full of people who want what you sell. All you have to do is pin the items you are selling to your boards and give an explanation of what it is and where they can get it.

The best way to gain followers is to maintain a dynamic board. Try to pin items frequently and always look for items that are interesting and eye catching. Search the internet for examples of afghans you like, pin links to how to web sites that explain how to crochet or offer free patterns. Always make sure the links are to web sites that are active. The worst thing to do is post an inactive link to nowhere.

Chapter 5 – Time to Stock the Shelves

If you are good there is money to be made, there are a few different ways to make money with your talent. With a little research you can find out what is in demand at the moment and if it is something you can make. Don't worry if you are not interested in making the "in" items, classics like afghans are always "in".

There are so many different crochet items to make, pot holders, coasters, holiday decorations, toys, pillows and shawls are just a few of the small items people like. The fun part is deciding what you want to make, with all of the choices this could take a while.

The best way to stock your store is to have several classic items that are always in demand, and then add a few of the popular items of the moment. For instance, afghans, baby items, pillows, and pot holders are some of the classic items that people like to buy, and amigurumi is a very popular crochet items at the moment. Try offering several of the classic items, then add a few different types of amigurumi and work from there.

Taking Special Orders: If you decide to take special orders, make sure you can give your customers an approximate time frame for completion. Your main goal is to keep customers happy, keeping them happy involves delivering on time. When you allow for custom orders, make sure you provide a form to fill out so you remember exactly what the customer asked for. Try and keep your special orders down to a few items, if you agree to take special orders on everything you sell, you will end up filling orders 24 and 7.

Your form for special orders will explain to the customer exactly what they are going to receive, when they will receive it, and an explanation of the special order itself. This is important so both you and the customer are on the same page.

What About Color: Many people will give advice about color, "stay neutral", "light colors sell better", the truth is, people look for items in colors that match their wardrobe and décor, you can't match everything, but you can take a look at what is selling and use those colors in the items you make. You can get color choices from fashion magazines, interior decorating magazines, and even TV commercials. Keep your eyes open and do a little research.

Special Note for Baby Items: If you plan to make crochet baby items, there are a few tips that will help you make sales and generate a profit.

- When making baby toys, embroider the eyes or any details there may be to avoid choking hazards
- Create equal colors for boys and girls and neutral colors as well
- Always use baby yarn for softness, touch, and feel

These are only suggestions that will help you avoid issues later on. Button eyes may look adorable on a crochet teddy bear but they can be a choking hazard. Even if they are sewn on with fishing string, babies will find a way to get them off that bear and into their mouth.

Baby items are the only items that require certain colors, blue for boys and pink for girls. Many people say that this is an old notion and color doesn't matter, but the first thing people say when asking about baby booties is "do they come in blue, she is having a boy". Do yourself a favor and keep equal amounts of both pink and blue, it will keep customers happy.

Conclusion

Now you know everything you need to know to start selling your wonderful crochet creations. Keep this book handy when you begin getting yourself started, it will come in handy as you open that store and stock those shelves. There is money to be made and now it's time for you to make some.

Remember you are an artist, try creating some of your own patterns, people love buying unique items. Write that blog! It is going to help you connect with your customers and help you make new ones. You may even end up surprising yourself with your blog and spark some creativity for new items.

Don't sell yourself short, remember, the crochet items you sell online have global reach. Utilize that amazing marketplace and sell everywhere with the click of a mouse. Your business can help you turn a profit and earn and help you make a living doing what you love.

Starting your own crochet business is not hard to do and it will bring you a feeling of satisfaction when you sell your first crochet creation. Nothing beats working for yourself, your skills and imagination are worth a pay check so get out there and start selling those beautiful creations!